Better, Not Busier: 7 Smart Hacks for Getting More Done with Less Stress

Disclaimer: This book provides general information intended for personal growth and educational purposes. It is not a substitute for professional advice. The authors assume no responsibility for any outcomes resulting from the use of the information contained herein.

Image Disclosure: All illustrations in this book were generated by the author using artificial intelligence (AI) tools.

First Edition: 2025

Dedication

To all of us who have at some point in our lives felt swamped with too much to do, too much to carry, and too much expectation from us, with inadequate energy to sustain it. Most individuals live with an invisible burden and, in most cases, may think that they have to work harder, extend longer, and demonstrate more. This book has been presented to you as a sweet reminder that your value is never based on overwork, and your value is never gauged by the amount of what you were able to get done in one day.

You need a balanced and clarity-oriented life. You are entitled to mornings that start with a serene mind, days that are planned around purpose, and evenings that end with a feeling of peace and not remorse. Hopefully, this book finds you at a time when you are willing to take a healthier step and are missing the room to breathe, think, sleep, and develop without feeling guilty.

May this content ease your burden and enable you to lose the habits that weaken you. May it guide you to discipline, which will bring glory to your health and uncover your real self. Most importantly, we hope each and every chapter will be reminding you that comfort is not a luxury, but a right, and that you deserve softness and rejuvenation in your life.

Preface

The notions in this book were discovered in the course of a long journey. We spent several years in the learning halls, full clinics, and overcrowded classes, observing people who have no time, energy, or hope left. We also experienced the same struggle in our lives. We worked harder, stretched ourselves out, and made efforts to live on very little sleep. Our thinking was that constant work was a test of discipline and commitment. But the more we pressed farther and further, the more fatigued we became. Productivity was like a moving target that was getting more and more distant every day.

It reached a turning point when it was revealed by psychology and organizational science that this was not true. Based on time management and self-regulation studies, well-being increases when individuals work with intention as opposed to pressure. Those in these disciplines define efficiency as clarity, focus, and balance, but not speed. We realized this and our view changed. We began to challenge our routines and reform the manner we planned, worked and slept. Minor alterations brought drastic results. That we should build sustainable success by design rather than by overwork.

We were inspired to write this book in order to share the discoveries that have changed our lives. We hope that our readers with different backgrounds will find simple and practical hacks that will help to save time, eliminate stress, and create high-impact habits. We also feel that knowledge is more powerful when it is shared. You are expected to think on these thoughts, apply them in your day-to-day life and share them with other people. When the majority of people work with comfort rather than struggle, society and working environments will be sounder and more human.

We hope that you will read this book with interest and an open mind. Try one hack at a time. See how little things make gradual improvements. Efficiency is not a particular gift to a few. It is something that you can train, use, improve and multiply. Hopefully, this book will lead you to a state of balance, clarity and a calmer mind.

— **Amro & Khalid**

Acknowledgment

We owe a debt of gratitude to numerous individuals who contributed in shaping up the ideas in this book and those who helped us along the way. Our families were a source of constant patience, understanding, and encouragement on our long writing days and late revisions. Their presence left us with a serene and emotional room that we required to think effectively and write with a meaning. They had responsibilities, reminded us of the need to sleep a bit and thought that this work was worth it even when the pages were not done.

Medicine and education also gave us a rich supply of ideas, on the part of our colleagues in these fields. Their stories, difficulties, and insights inspired a few chapters. Their stories demonstrated to us how individuals in any profession go through the same issues and seek healthier options to manage time, energy, and expectations. Also, the young professionals and students influenced the direction of this book. Their queries helped to tighten our explanations and the interest prompted us to dig deeper; their honesty made us realize where practical tools were most needed.

We affirm our love to the researchers whose work led our brains. Their research on productivity, habits, decision-making, and human behavior gave a good basis to each hack evidence in this book. We appreciate the mentors who made us understand that what truly matters is intent and not intensity, and that life is built on balance and not on speed.

Lastly, we do not disregard any reader who wants to gain clarity, balance, and well-being by reading through the pages of this book. Your journey matters. Your time matters. Your growth matters. We understand that you are giving us the privilege to follow you on your new habits, and to remodel your work and life orientation. Thank you: we got your attention and you've allowed us to introduce such ideas in your everyday lives. The fact that you are willing to pursue change is what makes this book really purposeful.

About the Authors

Amro Bin Abdulrahman

Amro Bin Abdulrahman is a scholarly director with a deep inclination towards human execution, education and a viable strategy toward individual performance. His work is a combination of research, teaching, and daily problem solving to assist people in developing healthier and more productive routines. He has helped students, young professionals, and working adults to overcome challenges posed by time, focus, and motivation. His teaching philosophy is focused more on clarity, balance and purpose, and less pressure and overload. Amro believes that efficiency increases when individuals plan their lives strategically and are aware of the practices that contribute to long-term health. His professional career and education enable him to articulate complicated concepts in very easy and practical terms. He still participates in education projects that help students and other professionals to acquire sustainable competencies, which enhance performance and quality of life. His objective is to ensure that people can work with ease and enjoy what they do in their day to day activities.

Khalid Bin Abdulrahman

Khalid Bin Abdulrahman is a seasoned professor and medical educator who has almost 30 years of experience in teaching, leadership, and improvement of organizations. He has been instrumental in the development of academic programs, enhancement of training systems, and leading of important educational and healthcare undertakings. His works are centered on smart planning, logical decisions and long term productivity under extreme stress. As a leader, Khalid has a purpose, teamwork, and vision-based leadership approach. His contribution on medical education continues to flow through the learning environments in areas that he has been able to influence policy and curriculum. He firmly adheres to ensuring that people and groups are made to work in a way that is not stressful; ensures that they are practiced in a balanced manner that reduces burnout and improves the performance. Teaching, mentoring, and involvement in research, make Khalid one of the driving forces of learners and professionals to develop meaningful habits and strive towards excellence with purpose and wellbeing at the core of the problem.

Table of Contents

Better, Not Busier: 7 Smart Hacks for Getting More Done with Less Stress

Chapter One: Introduction- The Foundation of Smart Productivity (Efficiency)

Each day starts off with hope. The alarm is on, the mind is alive and the day is full of possibilities. However, towards the end of the day, most professionals would be exhausted because of the tasks and messages that could not be answered at night. The contemporary world applauds movement and not necessarily improvement. We confuse action with success and hard work with effectiveness. The reality is quite straightforward, achievement does not mean doing much; it is doing what matters, well.

Figure 1.1: Balancing Efficiency and Effectiveness

Productivity is not overload, it is balance. Figure 1.1 above shows the tradeoff between doing things right (efficiency) and doing the right things (effectiveness). It demonstrates that sustainable productivity is based on the correlation of streamlined processes and meaningful goals.

Better, Not Busier was conceived in hospitals, in classrooms and boardrooms where work had become too much. At some point, the authors thought that more time equates to more dedication. As time went by, experience was found to be otherwise. Unrelenting schedules, full schedules, and perpetual multitasking did not result in excellence but rather fatigue. Balance without productivity causes burnout and not brilliance.

Efficiency lies in concentration, time, and relaxation. It makes disorder out of disorder and tension out of tension. Covey (2020) states that when people align their time with their very best values, they stand a chance to get more and better. Without purpose, the meaning of the structure is no longer there; it is scattered by effort.

Being a smarter worker does not imply being a less caring one. It is the more precise caring, which focuses its energy where it makes the difference. A teacher who is making plans, an engineer who has a design problem or a student who is exam planning what to do all have the same option; do you want to do it all or would it be better to keep the things that are necessary. Intentional effectiveness makes life clear.

Figure 1.2: Working Hard vs. Working Smart

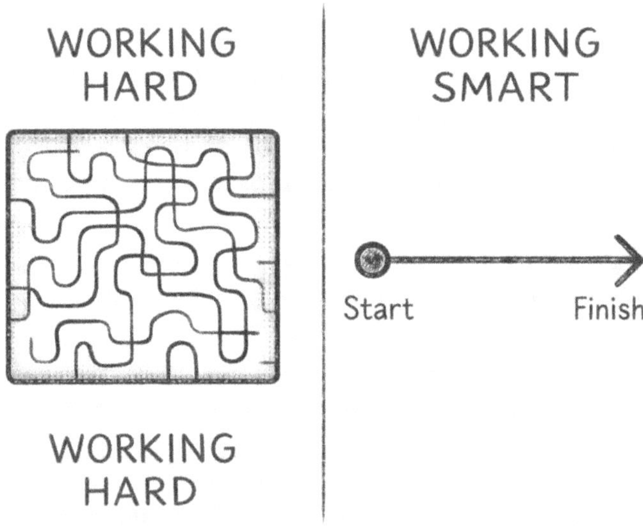

Strategy always outshines strain. The above image (figure 1.2) is a comparison of the ineffective complexity of working harder to the focused clarity of working smarter. It strengthens the fact that simplicity and strategy make more permanent productivity than strain and overwork.

Simplicity is essential to sustainable productivity. Complicated systems fail when the pressure is on, whereas simple routines are resistant to pressure. Small wins, time-blocking, and short reviews are designed to make a gradual progress. Mastery is a matter of reflection and not repetition. Once individuals strive towards less but more meaningful things they reconnect with tranquility and enthusiasm.

Research supports adoption of this attitude. Studies indicate that performance is enhanced when there are clear and quantifiable objectives. In the same way, Aeon et al. (2021) have shown that time management as a structured one can be used to reduce the level of stress and maximize satisfaction. It is clear in the science that we ought to pursue progress, and not perfection.

Energy is also respected in purposeful planning. The most successful professionals plan deep work at the optimal time of maximum alertness and then take a break. They know that as does any muscle the brain requires rhythm--strain and rest. Speed is not efficiency but sustainability.

Consider an example of a teacher called Sara who would prepare lessons even late at night. Her workload reduced and her lessons improved as she began to plan her most creative work in the morning and administrative grading in the evening. Her experience is a reflection of the central idea of this book: efficiency is created when effort is mixed with clarity.

Figure 1.3: Iceberg of Effort

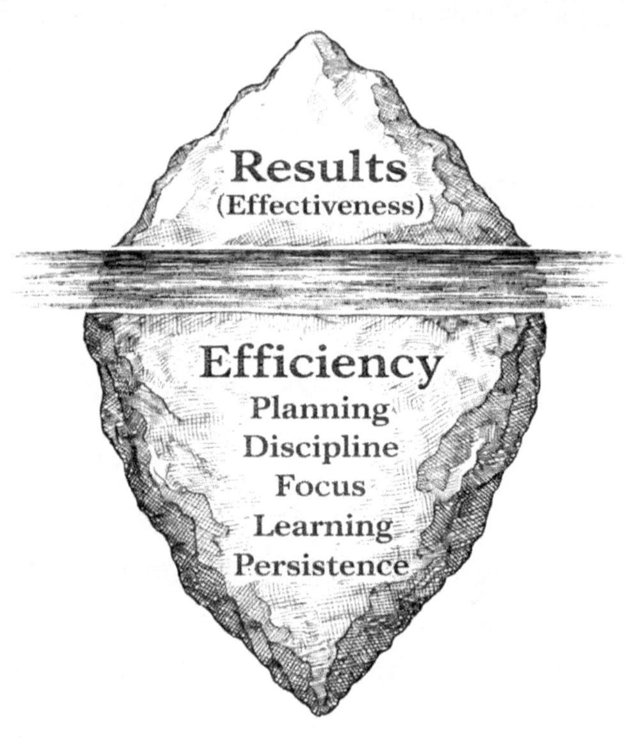

Figure 1.3 above illustrates that success is visible but it is based on invisible pillars like discipline, planning, and persistence. The bigger, unseen part is the symbol of the regular routines that keep success alive.

Success is a concept taught by what is perceived by humans on the view of things that are not being followed. All the success, apparently successful, is behind the scene: there is discipline, concentration and patience; but there are the silent habits, without which no real success is achievable. These are the non-visual production anchors. Success is the iceberg, as it was on the broad bottom of the iceberg; success is on the mute foundation of day-to-day routine.

Better, Not Busier encourages the readers to reconnect with this basis. The book is a blend of practical science and visual narration, which makes people reconsider their planning, priorities, and performance. It is not a guidebook of prohibitions but the path to clarity. The book provides one psychologically-based, yet practical, smart hack in each of the chapters which is backed by reflection exercises and graphic summaries.

Fundamentally, efficiency is an intentional philosophy. It involves creating time to think, innovate and rest. This book is meant to assist you to reclaim time not by filling your days with more stuff, but with creating meaningful days.

Reading this, you can only fathom exchanging messy schedules with a state of serenity, anxiety with reality, and exhaustion with progress. This is not a speed-up-and-get-busy goal but a get-better goal: conscious, calm and satisfied. Action doubles the efforts when there is purpose.

1.1 Shattering the Myth of "Working Harder"

Workers worldwide still perceive success in terms of working long hours, on call at all times and multitasking. The notion that hard work is an apt formula to success continues to afflict every professional culture. Nevertheless, the World Health Organization (2019) asserts that nowadays chronic overwork is the cause of burnout and the declining rates of work satisfaction. The working round the clock myth hides the reality that more hours do not always lead to better outcomes.

There is no linear relationship between the productivity and effort. The survey, carried out by the International Labour Organization (2022) throughout the globe revealed that jobs more than 48 hours a week are characterized by performance indices and even sub-optimal performance. Too much work decreases concentration of the mind, affects decision making quality and increases the errors. The case of karoshi death in Japan shows how costly the social element of equating time to success in Japan is (Artazcoz et al., 2013). This has also been noted in Europe and the Middle East whereby the working hours were found to be more in addition to stress and absenteeism.

The global economy is rewarding the creative, nimble and emotional intelligent and not just the enduring. Research shows that high-performing professionals do not work until they perform better but in order to perform better so that they can save time to focus and take breaks. Efficiency has ceased to be a luxury but an art that sets sustainable high performers apart and those who remain in the exhaustive cycles. The argument is presented, and it is that individuals can be more productive without necessarily having to work more; instead, it is a redesigning of how we use our time.

1.2 Understanding True Efficiency

The process begins with the efficacy of knowing the purpose and process. Effectiveness as Drucker (2006) explained refers to doing the right things, and efficiency doing things right. The two are imperative, but efficiency implies that work may lead to maximum good. On the organizational level, it is the ability to use small resources to achieve meaningful results. In my case, it is the fact that one can move on without straining.

Time management and goal alignment are motivating both productivity and health. Claessens et al. (2007) inferred that a strong correlation existed between job satisfaction and performance and structured time planning. Only recently, Aeon et al. (2021) confirmed that appropriate prioritizing and time management result in less stress and motivation. Yet time is one of the factors. Efficiency also incorporates efficiency in the way and attention as well as energy management. Schwartz and McCarthy (2007) demonstrated this by performing better when they made their schedules in accordance to natural energy cycles as compared to those who did not bother with rest and recovery.

The digital age is also a challenge added. Constant messages, online meetings and numerous emails interrupt its focus and ruin its efficiency. Koundal et al., (2024) state that a large amount of digital interruptions elevates the level of stress and deteriorates the quality of output. Attentions are thus rare resources of effective professionals. They create a borderline on the internet, schedules on setting-offs and leave weekends and holidays to accomplish complex jobs.

The other important key to efficiency is simplicity. Lean management principles which had been used initially in manufacturing can be applied in the individual productivity.

Unnecessary processes are cut, repetitive work is made to be on autopilot, and low-value processes are removed, which leaves free time to do high-impact activities. One example is that a manager who will utilize the digital dashboard tools rather than paper reports will save hours during a week, but on the other hand, a teacher who will use the automation of the forms to mark the work will save the time to develop lessons.

The multicultural working environments are universal concerning productivity. An example of a South African logistics firm that introduced lean operations has decreased the delivery time by a third, and a Saudi hospital that introduced a methodical shift setup reduced staff burnout and errors (Zayas-Cabán et al., 2022). These examples point to the fact that efficiency is better than culture; it is preoccupied with intelligent organization and sustainability of humans.

Efficiency is not mere mechanical optimization; it is thoughtful alignment between goals and effort. It is a replacement of being busy with being balanced, in disarray with being clear, and tired with being focused. As fast as technology, the fast workload around the world has become not a professional quality, but a necessity to be healthy. Working smart is also to re-possess the time, attention, and the purpose one is doing; the real antecedents of smart productivity.

Efficiency is therefore a daily choice. It requires discipline to focus, courage to simplify, and wisdom to pause. When individuals treat time deliberately as money, every task gains meaning. The smarter path is not faster; it is clearer.

Chapter 2: Hack 1 – Prioritize for Impact

2.1 Understanding the Eisenhower Matrix

In any business sector and in every culture, it is an everyday challenge for professionals to draw the distinction between the urgent and the really important. Physicians are working crazily to satisfy the needs of the patients, educators are doing administration paperwork and lesson planning, and business leaders are working in consecutive meetings with no room to breathe. Most of the time, individuals confuse being busy with being effective. Nonetheless, as Aeon et al. (2021) found in their meta-analysis of time management, one of the most chronic reasons for work-related stress and low performance is poor prioritization. Being busy and productive are two different aspects that can be distinguished by the fact that one must know what is really important and work towards it.

Figure 2.1: The Cognitive Process of Task Triage

The above picture (figure 2.1) demonstrates that deliberate choice helps to select tasks according to urgency and importance, which is useful in cognitive control and time management.

With the era of ubiquitous connectivity, it has become unclear where necessary and meaningless actions are. To professionals, it is possible to work hours responding to messages, conducting meetings, and replying to emails without having a significant change at the end of the day. This trend is indicative of a reactive but not a proactive mode of work. Cross et al. (2019) state that professionals dedicate over 85 percent of their week to collaborative demands, emails, meetings, and check-ins with little or no time to think strategically. The skill of prioritization has thus survived in the contemporary work culture.

The Eisenhower Matrix, or Urgent Important Matrix, is an age-old tool used to make effective and rational decisions. It originated with the principles of the decision-making process of U.S. President Dwight D. Eisenhower and was subsequently modified by productivity researchers as an effort to balance urgency and importance to create four quadrants of tasks. The categories are as follows.

Figure2.2: Eisenhower Matrix

The matrix above (figure 2.2) breaks down tasks into four categories: Do, Decide, Delegate, and Delete, which assists people in distinguishing between what is urgent and what is really important.

1. **Important and Urgent (Quadrant I: Do).** These are those tasks that are crisis or deadline-driven (for example, medical emergency, project due date, customer complaint), or require immediate attention.
2. **Not Urgent but Important (Quadrant II: Decide).** The activities create success in the long run and avoid crises. These are strategic planning, professional learning, preventive maintenance, and relationship-building.
3. **Urgent and Not Important (Quadrant III: Delegate).** These activities seem urgent yet add minimal value, for example, unnecessary meetings, regular reports, or disruptions created by the priorities of other people.
4. **Not urgent and not important (Quadrant IV: Delete).** These distractions are of minimal or no help like too much social media, gossiping, or unnecessary administration.

Effective prioritization consists of focusing the majority of the time on Quadrant II. In this category are activities that enable systems and relationships to be strengthened before they turn into a crisis. Research conducted by Harvard Business Review, the performance of high-performing professionals is specifically supported by the conscious setting aside of time to perform activities in Quadrant II (Cross et al., 2019). To illustrate, they set up strategic check-ups prior to escalation of problems, exercise routinely to keep up with energy, and invest in professional learning prior to the emergence of skill gaps. Comparatively, individuals whose lives are mainly in Quadrant I, the urgent zone are constantly on the reaction mode, which more often than not, leads to burnout.

Psychologically, prioritization is related to the executive function theory that can be used to explain how the brain is able to plan, contain impulses and control goals (Miyake & Friedman, 2012). The executive function enables one to take breaks, consider options, and rationally distribute energy. Individuals who have better executive control are less successful in being distracted and time-pressed. Likewise, Locke and Latham's (2019) argue that people with hierarchies of goals do better as they are able to notice which actions are related to their primary goals and eliminate the rest.

Aeon et al. (2021) noted that managing time is not only a behavioral skill, but it is also a psychological control process. The most productive employees are those who use time carefully among objectives and are conscious of where their focus is. They also take charge of what is worthy of attention, as opposed to the day being predetermined by outside forces.

2.1.1 Prioritization in the Digital Age

The digital revolution has increased both the opportunity and the distraction. Even nowadays, a person in the profession encounters hundreds of messages and notifications; mail, WhatsApp, Slack, and project managers. These systems make it possible to be connected, but they lead to fragmentation in attention. Research by Koundal et al. (2024) found that the digital interruption diminishes the capacity of deep work by as much as 40 percent, along with an increase in the level of stress. Repetitive change of tasks produces mental exhaustion, slows down decision-making, and predisposes to mistakes.

Consequently, the Eisenhower Matrix can be used not only to improve productivity but also to act as a type of cognitive defense against digital overload. Those who embrace digital minimalism, dedicating time to email once a week, turning off nonessential notifications, and proclaiming communication-free time, say their concentration is improved and their feelings are elevated. This is the approach that has been taken systematically by many organizations. As an example, a Saudi hospital has launched the use of digital dashboards, which use the Eisenhower Matrix to assist medical teams in prioritizing daily tasks. In six months, the efficiency scores increased, and employees said they were less stressed.

The technology can help in prioritizing, but may also overpower prioritization. The Eisenhower principle is efficiently implemented by professionals in their digital space with filters of importance, which is, categorizing emails in terms of their project value or urgency. Wajcman (2019) explains that such selective application of technology is an indication of a new kind of digital discipline whereby people take charge of technology rather than the other way around.

2.1.2 Cross Culture Dimensions of Prioritization

Although the Eisenhower Matrix is universal logic, it is applied differently in different cultures. Collectivist societies such as East Asia, Africa and Middle East have social harmony as a priority and then time discipline is not a priority in this kind of society. Incivility can be regarded as turning down a request. Hofstede (2011) defines the culture of high context as not emphasizing on strict time schedules but laying more emphasis on relationships and duties. Such professionals in such situations consequently adjust prioritization by applying polite deferral methods instead of direct refusal.

In the county administration offices in Kenya, for instance, time-map combined with respectful communication techniques were adopted by managers who initiated so-called priority scheduling sessions. Employees were taught to respond to non-urgent requests by saying, "I appreciate your job, and will do it after the main objective is achieved during this day." In three months, productivity was enhanced without ruining work relations. In the same manner, the Japanese project leaders tend to put the task delays in their group achievement and focus on sequencing over speed to ensure that the group stays together without losing focus.

Western cultures of organization, on the contrary, focus on personal freedom and quantifiable results. The employees are advised to say no to work with low priority and guard their focus time. Nonetheless, the globalization of the world presupposes that most teams combine both models. Good prioritizing must thus be culturally sensitive: the capacity to find a balance between individual productivity and social peace.

2.1.3 The Psychology of Saying "No"

The failure of prioritization is usually not related to the inability of people to have access to the tools, but rather to the fear of disappointing others. Research by Baumeister and Heatherton (1996) reveal that self-regulation is a restricted source of psychology that depletes when there is an emotional burden. Over-committers are exhausted in terms of their cognitive energy, and they also prove to be reactive. The art of saying no positively teaches one to regain control of oneself and get down to serious business.

The professionals will be able to put refusals in a positive perspective: they can explain priorities when refusing a request. An example is when someone says, "I would love to help, but I am putting together the quarterly report now." This neither negates value nor crosses boundaries. This is consistent with the evidence provided by Cross et al. (2019), who discovered that high performers control the intensity of collaboration through the selective nature of high-value interactions.

2.1.4 Strategic Time Allocation

The opportunity cost principle is also associated with the Eisenhower Matrix; an hour spent doing a low-impact activity is one hour spent that would be used doing a high-impact activity. This is referred to as strategy time allocation within the realm of management science. To the scholars, time is nonrenewable compared to money; how time is spent is an act of values and priorities.

Prioritization models have been incorporated in the performance reviews of the major companies. Managers do not merely judge what employees are doing, but also how they are allocating attention in an effective manner. As an indication, Lim (2023) quotes that the leaders who dedicate at least 40 percent of their week to the long-term strategic activity show better performance in comparison with leaders who pay a small to no attention to urgent issues.

2.1.5 The Essence of Quadrant II Thinking

In the Eisenhower Matrix, Quadrant II represents important but not urgent activities, which are planning, reflection, and learning. It is the area of prevention and development, where the professionals are proactive and not reactive. The core of the Eisenhower philosophy is quadrant II, the sphere of the important and not urgent work. Time payback in this case is exponential. It prevents crisis, develops creativity and encourages future growth. The Quadrant II implies reflection, learning, and prevention, the back story to the seeming success. Nonetheless, it is the quadrant that is very easily ignored because it demands an outlook and not a response. The people do not plan but re-act to the present as Drucker (2006) admitted.

It requires discipline, courage and consciousness to build Quadrant II habit. It must also be realized that strategy-less efficiency will be mere rapidity in the direction of irrelevance. Those professionals who are able to master Quadrant II thinking experience less stress and are more satisfied. They lose the value of themselves not on what they can do but upon the impact of what they desire to do. This mood is the basic foundation of productive sustainability in the contemporary world of digitization, which is also becoming globalized.

2.2 True-to-Life Scenario: The Prioritization Story

Amira is a 35-year old Riyadh based project manager who was a very daring, admired individual regarding her responsiveness and dedication. She would reply to emails promptly, never missed any meeting and never missed a call. However, her long hours never helped her out, as all her projects were perpetually behind schedule. Her employer described her as working, but not causing a difference. The harder Amira attempted, the weaker she became. At least she was stuck in a vicious circle of fatigue.

This transformed her after she was sponsored by her firm to take a leadership course on strategic productivity. The training introduced her to the Eisenhower Matrix, which is a decision-making model that distinguishes between urgent and important things. The idea sounded simple but gave a good deal of maternal indulgence in her manners. Amira performed self-audit process within the span of one week to ascertain that her 70 percent time was consumed in Quadrant III activities; urgent but not important activities such as unnecessary approvals and repetitive follow-ups. Less than one out of ten percent of her time was under Quadrant II; planning, strategy and growth.

This imbalance is common. Evidence shows that all employees in the world have over 50 percent of their time in control of their work and not working, which are also characterized by meetings and responding to emails. Psychologists refer to this tendency of comparing action to progress as action bias. Amira was a reactive and not a strategic worker, as most professionals are.

Amira employed the Eisenhower approach in her schedule with the help of a coach. In the morning she commenced with strategy and analysis blocks, in which she was the most wakeful. Timely communication was altered to short afternoons. She had learned to respond rudely in a nice way when interrupted: "I would like to help but I first have to finish my major job."

First, she feared being considered as being unhelpful but the results altered her perceptions. The team of Amira met the milestones in a timely manner, the level of efficiency increased by 25 percent, and stress levels were reduced in three months. Evenings at home and sleep were also regained by her.

The experience she gained confirms the findings of Aeon et al. (2021) who have realized that employees who are more mindful of the time they spend openly report improved levels of emotional well-being and achieve more objectives. Employment of prioritization does not enhance productivity alone; it restores balance and significance.

The experiences of Amira show a change in thinking about work across the world to bc smarter. The Eisenhower model was applied by a Kenyan nonprofit making organization in the field of health in order to reduce the amount of time spent on administrative report writing. With a primary focus on community outreach

(Quadrant II), vaccination coverage increased by 20 percent in six months, whereas over time it decreased (Terefe et al., 2023).

On the same note, one of the Canadian technology start-ups launched the Quadrant II Fridays, where time was allocated to innovation and process learning. Their software mistakes were reduced, and productivity was increased by 18 percent. Both scenarios demonstrate that making the important but not urgent is better to improve the organizational outcomes and the employees' satisfaction.

Amira is psychologically heading into the self-regulation theory. Self-regulation also helps a person to resist the short-term temptations and stay with the long-term goals as explained by Baumeister and Heatherton (1996). It is not merely willpower but a good exploitation of mental resources. These resources are used up when it is always in the form of reactivity and are saved in the structured focus.

This process is facilitated by neuroscience. Heatherton (2021) found that recurring attention reinforces brain networks related to executive control, which makes it simpler to screen out distractions. The priorities that are achieved with time redefine the behavior at a neurological level, making discipline the norm. Boundaries are a second nature to Amira, and that is why she would be calm in stressful situations.

Organizational culture was also evidenced by the challenge that Amira faced. Responsiveness rather than results was compensated by her company. Those employees who responded quickest were commended despite their shallow output. Such cultures get speed mixed up with efficiency. Wajcman (2019) states that in the contemporary work setting, visibility is often rewarded instead of being valued to encourage continuous busyness. Amira started to shield her attention, which was misunderstood by some of her colleagues. Nonetheless, the improvement of results led to a realization of her approach by the management as an example of results rather than responsiveness.

Her change was also influenced by the cultural context. The saying of “no” can be taken as disrespectful in the collectivist societies in Africa, the Middle East, and Asia. Research by Hofstede (2011) reveal that these cultures give more emphasis to harmony and a sense of belonging to a group rather than time. Amira modified and employed deferrals of respect and not refusals. Her courteous words, “Can we go over this later?” were efficient and understanding at the same time. This cross-culturally aware assertiveness preserved associations and secured her priorities.

The more Amira remained faithful to her, the larger the number of people she changed. Her staff started operating under the identical pattern and every week, they had a meeting to arrange the operations as revealed by Eisenhower Matrix. The meetings have been replaced by responsive updates, under which the scheduled conversations occur. It led to the team coincidence, which is associated with the effectiveness of work in the team when prioritization according to low turnover and prioritization were implemented.

Amira resembles a typical reality of being hectic and unproductive and the vast majority of the professionals are highly technical and do not know how to select the location where to invest their energies. The overtime work in the Quadrant I leads to burnout, loss of focus by working in Quadrant IV, and as a matter of fact, the real development falls within Quadrant II; the world of vision, innovation and development.

Months after Amira was transformed, she began mentoring new employees. Her Eisenhower chart was reviewed each Monday by her and her team and she explained why she made the priorities the way she did. Her calmness and keenness to detail was motivating. It was a leader who had clarity and this was the difference between this previously beaten manager and a leader.

The Amira story brings out a very critical truth that it is not the hard working people who are successful, but the people working with a purpose. The Eisenhower Matrix helped her and many others similar to her to get off the reactive to the planning levels, busyness to the impact levels. It has been proved that through global evidences that organizations that train teams to draw the line between urgency and importance are long term productive, less burned and more resilient. In a world whereby individuals are always being informed and bombarded with digital noise, prioritization is not only a professional tool, but also a way towards meaningful living.

2.3 Actionable Steps to Prioritize Your Day

When prioritization is turned into reality, it makes sense. Specifically, Cross et al. (2019) note that by planning their day ahead, professionals have to achieve more with minimal stress compared to other professionals who respond to situations as they appear. Prioritization is not dependent on strict scheduling that is done on a daily basis; prioritization is about matching effort with impact. The evidence-based measures below will make the Eisenhower Matrix a daily routine for a productive and peaceful mind.

Figure 2.3: The Urgency Trap and Cognitive Overload

Figure 2.3 above illustrates that the perpetual sense of urgency causes cognitive overload and decreases the quality of performance. It points out the psychological price of multitasking and the need to consciously prioritize to stay focused and mentally clear.

2.3.1 Start with the "Big Three"

Start every morning by making decisions on the three key tasks that are going to propel your goals. These are not the little things or your fast responses, but are high-impact tasks that make your day or break it. Aeon et al. (2021) discovered that the concentration on a limited set of outcomes enhances accomplishing tasks and personal satisfaction as it concentrates cognitive energy in making progress. These three priorities put on paper or digital planner transform intent into tangible action. Individuals who treat these things as non-negotiable usually describe a greater feeling of control and a decrease in anxiety.

Figure 2.4: The Most Important Task (MIT) Strategy

The diagram above (Figure 2.4) shows that intention is converted into action by identifying and accomplishing the top three priorities of the day. It focuses on putting energy in high impact activities that can give quantifiable progress.

The Big Three principle is applicable in practice in any profession. One teacher can work on the development of one effective lesson plan, use feedback from students, and prepare an inspection. A project manager can focus on revising a proposal, chairing an important meeting, and addressing one of the operating problems. What matters is clarity. Starting the day with set goals will render the distractions useless since you know what you need to achieve.

2.3.2 Get Tricky with the Eisenhower Quadrants

The Eisenhower Matrix is still among the easiest but the most effective ways to organize a to-do list. Once you are aware of the Big Three, assign other tasks by quadrant using the four quadrants of importance and urgency. Professionals who are consciously grouping tasks devote more time to Quadrant II, the long-term growth and strategy area.

Work on Quadrant II should be the first (planning, building relationships, and innovation). Such are the activities that do not necessarily have a strict deadline but the most serious long-term implications. The second step is dealing with Quadrant I: the immediate and serious matters which may not be postponed. Quick but not serious activities, like quadrant III, need to be outsourced or automated. Finally, minimize Quadrant IV distracters; browsing the internet, spam, or unnecessary conferences.

You learn to be aware of your time allocation by putting daily tasks on paper. Asana or Notion are digital tools that might help in prioritizing planning, but they must be easy to access (not cluttered) and only simplify the process. Research shows that it is true that technology, which complicates organization too much, will result in false productivity; activity without value.

Figure 2.5: The ABCDE Prioritization Ladder

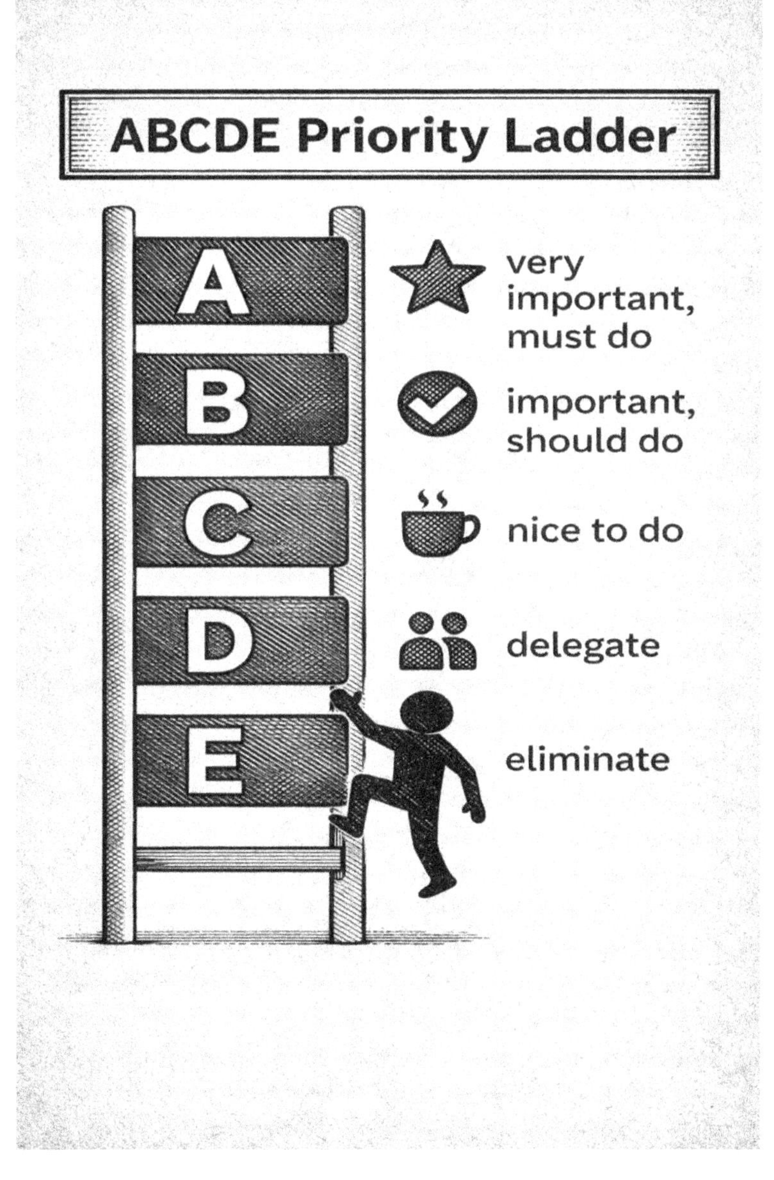

This ladder (figure2.5) shows the prioritization of tasks A (critical) to E (eliminate). It supports the fact that prioritization that is organized lowers overload and directs the effort to the highest-valued tasks in the long run.

2.3.3 Batch and Block Time

Task switching is often exhaustive and lowers the quality of output. The explanation behind this is switching costs, which refers to the time that is wasted when the brain has to reorient towards a new activity (Koch et al., 2018). In order to minimize this loss, similar tasks should be grouped together and then done in time blocks. Examples of these can include responding to emails at 11 a.m. and 4 p.m. instead of responding throughout the day. Calls should be scheduled as a block rather than scattered throughout the hours.

Time blocking establishes psychological aspects of protection against focus. As an example, using structured blocks leads the workers to do more tasks with less overall time. Discipline is also reinforced due to blocks, which make priority appointments with oneself. Interruptions also reduce automatically when you schedule two hours of deep work and make it a meeting.

2.3.4 Guard Your Peak Hours

The concentration of human beings varies throughout the day. The majority of adults have the optimal cognitive performance level during a two to four-hour natural alertness. Saving these choice hours of valuable deep and detailed work rather than management will be a long way to significant productivity enhancement.

Morning time is the most fruitful to the majority. Even the late evenings could be more fruitful to other people, especially the creative professionals. The trick is to find your rhythm and synchronize it with the most strenuous work. People should not schedule meetings, emails, or anything reactive during these high-energy periods (Schwartz & McCarthy, 2007). Work intensity means matching the intensity of work with the intensity of the biological energy, thus saving time and allowing you to work on your business less often, and eliminating mental exhaustion.

2.3.5 Review and Reflect Daily

Experience is converted into learning through reflection. Take ten minutes at the end of the day to review what you accomplished and what a waste of time was. You should ask yourself, "Did I concentrate on something important?" Goal clarity and reduction of emotional exhaustion are enhanced by short, structured reflection.

Reflection is also a strong motivational effort on the following day. By appreciating how well you are progressing, even with slight gains, your brain rewards productive behavior, releasing dopamine. On the other hand, distractions can be detected and corrected before they develop into a habit. The majority of workers have a priority journal in which they write down their daily Big Three and check them off. As weeks go by, a trend will be drawn that will indicate the best place to invest time and energy.

2.3.6 Say "No" Strategically

Studying to refuse unnecessary demands is the key to prioritization. Baumeister and Heatherton (1996) explain that self-control is like a muscle; it becomes weak when overworked. Individuals who keep assenting to the demands of others experience decision fatigue and are no longer focused on their personal goals. Refusal at the strategic level is not egocentric, as it maintains integrity and effectiveness.

In very social or collectivist societies, a no should be said in a subtle manner. Professionals can use polite deferral language, such as "I am busy on an important project but can help you later in the week." This will maintain relations while keeping the focus. Teams that uphold respectful management of boundaries report high levels of trust as well as reduced burnout.

2.3.7 Schedule Recovery Time

Contrary to common knowledge, rest is as important a factor in productivity as effort. Constant working leaves one's attention and emotional stability drained. Albulescu et al. (2022) also proved that when employees experience planned micro-breaks, short stretching, hydration, or deep breathing breaks, they are more engaged and make fewer mistakes. Brief rest periods re-energize the executive aspect of the brain, which enhances the quality of decisions.

Other than breaks, total rest entails adequate sleep, physical exercises and communication. The authors have emphasized the importance of such management of one's energy- physical, emotional, and mental- instead of time analysis or management (Schwartz and McCarthy, 2007). This happens because rest is introduced systematically in the day and thus more creativity and patience. The renewal period planners will be much stronger to pressure and they will not burnout too readily.

2.3.8 End with Intention

After the end of your working day, bring back your list and organize the following morning Big Three. Pre-planning approach will reduce the stress in the morning and the mind will not think about work during rest days. Heatherton (2021) explains that the neural loops that contribute to emotional regulation and decision making are optimized by the mental repetitions and as time passes, prioritization becomes a habit; an attitude and not a challenge.

These steps go hand in hand when they are practiced regularly, for instance, you wake up in the morning with a positive mind, concentrate on your work, say no with ease, sleep without feeling guilty and retire at the end of the day. What will come out of it is increased productivity and a more directed, peaceful life.

Prioritization is eventually a state of mind. Every minor decision: to concentrate, to ponder, to sleep compounds accrued power of control over the expenditure of time and energy that one has. Drucker (2006) noted that efficiency is doing things right, and effectiveness is doing the right things. The act of prioritization that is done daily helps you to do both.

2.4 Workbook Reflection: Apply the Hack

Take ten minutes to perform a *Priority Audit*.

1. Write down everything you did yesterday.
2. Mark each item as urgent, important, both, or neither.
3. Identify one Quadrant II task you neglected and schedule it this week.
4. Identify one Quadrant III task you can delegate or drop.
5. Observe how your energy and focus shift when you act on these changes.

Always keep in mind that prioritization is does not depend on doing everything perfectly, it is about devoting to what is important the best you can. It is not the quantity of tasks that should be done but the importance of the ones that are held.

2.5 Chapter Summary

Priority is the most important notion of smart productivity. It renders a chaotic effort meaningful since one concentrates on everything that is important. Data includes confirmation that the Eisenhower Matrix is a potent tool that can be capable of facilitating the distinction between the urgent needs and the important long-term objectives as the tool of making the professionals concentrate on responsive working, as opposed to proactive and transformative to their performance. The chapter has presented a real life case study of Amira in showing how individuals are able to enhance their performance, reduce stress and restore balance by formulating strategic decisions as to which tasks to do and which tasks to avoid.

Identifying the Big Three, time blocks, guarding the peak hours, and reflecting on the day are all the ways of prioritization each day that makes the theory a habit. According to Cross et al.

(2019), the prioritization strategy establishes and improves productivity and well-being, and Aeon et al. (2021) verify that the time management directed towards the achievement of meaningful goals has a positive influence on satisfaction and burnout.

The ability to say no politely, manage online distractions, and concentrate on business purposes is a current career success in all regions around the world, in Riyadh, Africa, or Toronto. Prioritizing does not imply doing more but doing better what is correct. When such principles are put to practice on a daily basis, then individuals gain a momentum of focus, energy and clarity; the attributes that sustain performance and create an indelible impression in the work place and in life.

Key Takeaways

- Prioritization makes a difference between being busy and being productive.
- The Eisenhower Matrix is useful in isolating importance and urgency.
- Daily Big three tasks are simple and do not cause too much.
- Reflection reinforces consciousness, and it develops continuous attention.
- Strategic no responding saves on time and energy.

Weekly Challenge

1. Select your three daily Big Three, and list them morning by morning.
2. Rank your present to-do list according to the Eisenhower Matrix.

3. Deep or continuous work for two hours.
4. Always remember to say no, in a polite manner once assigning a non-urgent task.
5. At the end of the day: observe: what was important, what was not important.

Chapter 3: Hack 2 – Plan with Purpose

The key to any successful endeavor is that it must have a clear plan that bridges the gap between intention and action. Allen (2015) asserts that planning is the gap between vision and execution. When people are strategic, they focus their efforts on things that matter rather than responding to daily stress.

The contemporary working environment is full of uncertainty and thus it has been seen that it results in reactive decision making and wastage of time. Intentionality assists people in acting strategically rather than acting on the spur of the moment.

The point of purposeful planning is not to have elaborate timetables but to come up with plans that are adaptable, understandable and align with personal values. Follow-through and consistency are highly enhanced by having clear plans that define when, where, and how things will be done as Oettingen and Gollwitzer (2010) argue. Planning helps in converting unclear goals into specific actions that are time bound.

Nevertheless, planning has been confused with perfectionism whereby most individuals take more time to make plans than implement them. Planning with purpose aims at making execution simple and promoting discipline.

Planning with balance between clarity and flexibility is equally beneficial to professionals in other professions, such as teachers, engineers, healthcare workers, or artists. By making time and acting intentionally, people regain their time, alleviate anxiety, and generate space to be creative. The subsequent sections discuss how to formulate actionable plans, prevent over-planning, learn real-life contrasts, and use evidence-based practical tips in planning.

3.1 Crafting Clear and Actionable Plans

Planning changes the possibility into development. People who make specific and measurable goals have a much greater chance of success compared to those who use vague intentions. A well-defined strategy will transform aspiration into a set of actions that are realistic.

In the many organizations, individuals fail due to their goals not being structured. Planning is what defines what will be done, when it will be done, and how it will be done, and makes sure that each step has a purpose.

Figure 3.1: If-Then Bridge

Figure 3.1 above illustrates that the planning of if-then facilitates the process of closing the gap between intention and achievement. An extensive meta-analysis has discovered that the development of particular implementation intentions is a significant enhancement of goal achievement in health, academic, and professional settings.

Psychologists suggest that this process happens via the concept of implementation intentions. Gollwitzer and Sheeran (2006) argue that implementation intentions bridge the gap between intention and behavior in the use of the if-then statements, for instance, "When it is 9 a.m., then I will start the weekly report."

These little, pre-programmed actions turn intention into behavior automatically. Those who use this model develop regular habits that turn motivation into outcomes. Goal-focused planning, in turn, creates habits that simplify the focus and quicken the decision-making process.

Figure 3.2: Automatic Goal Pursuit

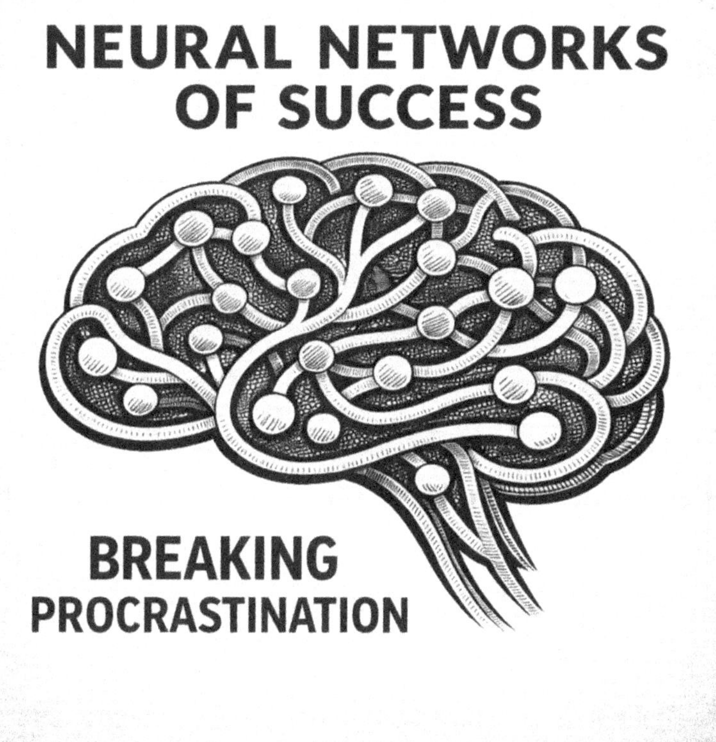

Figure 3.2 above shows that implementation intentions enhance associative networks that promote automatic goal pursuit. Empirical studies indicate that such cue-response associations affect cognitive load and increase follow through.

Technology is now significant in organized planning. Mazmanian et al. (2013) state that digital tools like Todoist, Trello, or Notion are used to serve human purposes and organize complicated workloads but not to control them. When professionals are guided by digital reminders blindly, they tend to lose focus. Intentional application of such tools helps to focus and organize. An example is a nurse in Manila, who can only use a simple digital checklist in planning the patient rounds, making sure there are short breaks to avoid fatigue. Such micro-planning keeps the performance and emotional condition high.

Intentional planning starts by determining what is more important. Covey (2020) called them the big rocks, the most important goals that need to be placed in the schedule of the person before other minor ones. Professionals who have significant goals do not waste time on distractions. An example would be a teacher who is about to administer final exams and plans to grade early in the week and have a later session where he/she provides personalized student feedback. This way of prioritization ensures that focus is directed towards activities that create the highest value.

Time-blocking is another important component of actionable planning. Breaking down the day into blocks of structured focus would help to avoid decision fatigue and task switching. Intentional planners group together similar tasks to conserve the mental energy.

Parke et al.'s (2018) study revealed that time-blocking enhances attention capacity and decreases mental load. A designer can spend mornings at work and afternoons on emails or meetings. This practice enhances focus as it matches the level of energy with the requirements of the tasks.

Achievement is also increased through backward planning which starts with the end in mind. Freund and Hennecke (2015) state that the final goal can be visualized to rationally allocate the time and resources. As an illustration, an architect in Singapore drawing up a project submission can begin by determining the final approval date and then backtrack to give deadlines on concept sketches, design reviews and final modifications. This will decrease the pressure of the last-minute modifications and provide a steady progress.

There should also be reflection checkpoints in the effective plans. Weekly reviews are useful to allow people to assess progress, identify challenges and modify objectives. Reflection helps routines not to be fixed and be out of touch with the reality. It also develops flexibility- a key characteristic in the modern work environment which is very fast-paced. Reflection helps planners to review their outcomes and keep on refining their plans.

Another basis of purposive planning is simplicity. Clear (2018) states that simple plans are easy to maintain and implement. Complicated schedules do not encourage follow-through as they require excessive mental work. Professionals should focus on three key objectives per day. It is better to get a handful of meaningful tasks done to gain momentum and not to make a list full of clutter that is only going to cause fatigue. A brief, goal-oriented plan brings motivation and confidence.

The cross-cultural evidence is supporting the universality of structured planning. In the Gulf region, employees who had daily plans, which were structured, had higher satisfaction levels, and much lower burnout rates. On the same note, Indian teachers who employed micro-planning enhanced performance in the classroom and adjusted to hybrid learning more easily. These illustrations show that there are certain principles of planning that are applicable in various cultural and professional environments.

Energy management is also important in actionable planning. To achieve sustainable productivity, one must schedule his or her activities in accordance with the natural energy cycles. Intentional strategists plan intricate activities in high-energy seasons and abandon routine work to slower times. This biological correspondence increases concentration and minimizes fatigue. In the case of an engineer, one can work on analytical calculations in the morning and administrative reports in the afternoon, and the amount of work corresponds to the energy expended.

Purposeful planning is not simply a matter of time organization but a matter of planning focus. Aeon et al. (2021) explain that time management is most effective in the context of goal clarity and self-reflection. A plan that simply enumerates activities will not guarantee purpose. The best planners thus consider the reasons why something is important and the way it is relevant to bigger goals. They develop intrinsic motivation by relating daily activities to the long-term sense.

Actionable planning is enhanced by feedback loops. The tracking of progress causes the feeling of momentum, which strengthens commitment, as Amabile and Kramer (2011) explain. Documenting small victories on a daily or weekly basis makes professionals feel that they are getting results. This creates a sense of psychological fulfillment and drives one to persevere even in hard stages. An example of a marketing professional following campaign milestones is that he or she remains interested as he or she can see the progress being made.

Accountability is also enhanced in the present day workplaces through collaborative planning. Group planning software, group schedules, and group progress boards can assist people in aligning themselves with group objectives. Bakker and Demerouti (2017) state that transparent planning enhances coordination and eliminates role conflict in teams. Work is less stressful when everybody knows about the common timeframe and the major goals.

Lastly, intentional planning entails flexibility. No plan survives unchanged. Grant and Parker (2009) propose that effective planners consider plans as living documents that change as they receive new information. Plans that are the most effective are organized and at the same time not rigid and can be adjusted without bringing about havoc. When a worker is confronted with an unexpected situation like the urgent client request, he/she can rearrange priorities in a short time when he/she has already planned to have buffer time in case of an emergency.

The art of making action plans thus involves science, discipline, and self-awareness. It starts with specific objectives, proceeds with a planned implementation, and is adaptable enough to adapt to the uncertainty. Intentional planners understand that planning does not imply control but guidance. They put goals in simple steps, use energy wisely and often reflect to become better. Covey (2020) state that good planning is not dependent on time management but focus management. Ultimately, the art of intentional planning is to create meaningful progress, rather than ideal schedules.

3.2 Avoiding Over-planning and Perfectionism

Over planning conceals itself behind the guise of discipline. It is confused with dedication by many professionals, which is time-consuming and performance-degrading. Stoeber and Otto (2006) state that perfectionism usually masquerades as ambition but results in anxiety and inefficiency.

Over-planners take more time planning how to do things than on what they want to do. Their strategies are hindrances rather than instruments of improvement. Psychologists refer to this trend as procrastinatory perfectionism, the habit of delaying the work until things are just right. Regrettably, such ideal conditions are not common.

Figure 3.3: Daily Time Distribution

Figure 3.3 above illustrates the allocation of focus work, breaks, meetings and wasted time. Longitudinal and experimental research has shown that proactive scheduling and time-blocking enhance sustained attention and reduce cognitive fatigue.

Avoidance behaviors are triggered by fear of imperfection. The human brain finds a way of comforting itself by postponing difficult tasks and justifying that there is more to be prepared. But over preparation is just more tension building. The similarity between over-planning and under-planning is that they both lead to stress with no improvements. Hence, intentional planning involves moderation, a well-planned system that is not too rigid to change with time.

The good enough rule is one of the effective strategies that can be used against perfectionist planning. Satisficers (who are satisfied with satisfactory results) are more satisfied and productive than maximizers (who pursue perfection).

As an example, a university lecturer in Kuala Lumpur writing online lectures can complete his/her slides after the communication of the main points is made rather than spending a couple of days in changing colors or fonts. This minor change of mind spares time and energy on other more important activities like interactive teaching and student response.

Another practical way of overcoming over-planning is time boxing. It is an activity where certain activities are allocated specific time and one promises to cease the activity when time elapses. This strategy makes planning an action. It shifts the emphasis on perfection to progress and curtails the never-ending process of revisions. Professionals who time-box claim to be more accountable and less distracted due to the fact that deadlines create movement.

Emotional insecurity frequently results in over-planning. A lot of people associate self-worth with perfect results. They are afraid of starting work that might expose them to fault or criticism. Intentional planning transforms this ideology by making success consist of consistency rather than perfection.

All unsuccessful attempts are a part of the evolution. Professionals that adopt an iterative planning process of plan, act, review, and adjust, proceed. They are happy to know that plans are not pre-planned but evolve as time goes by.

The other current form of over-planning is the information overload. In the cyberspace where information is an overload, people spend too much time conducting research before making a choice. Heavy information-seeking decrease task completion by over 30 percent. Careful strategists draw limits to the gathering of information.

As an example, a startup pitch deck organizer in Seoul can focus on two confirmed market reports rather than reading endless materials on the Internet. This limitation brings about focus, acceleration in decision making, and momentum.

Cognitive resources are also exhausted in over-planning. Willpower is finite and it can be depleted through excessive initial choices. Planning is complex and it consumes mental energy prior to the execution of the plan. Streamlined rituals guard such energy.

Allen (2015) proposed the two-minute rule that suggests doing any task that can be finished within less than two minutes instead of scheduling it. These micro-actions liberate the brain to work on high-value and complex objectives. Intentional strategists realize that structure must be energy giving rather than energy consuming.

The ultimate cure to perfectionism is adaptability. Flexible planners are more satisfied and more successful in the long term than inflexible planners. Flexible planning enables prompt rectification of difficulties. In the health sector, such as at the emergency room, physicians work on a structured triage system and switch immediately when new patients show up. Success is pegged on their ability to be flexible and operate within a stable framework. This model is a reflection of the coexistence of structure and responsiveness in the purposeful planning.

Mindfulness supplements flexibility. Creswell (2017) argues that mindful awareness helps to reduce anxiety about the future by focusing on the present. By thinking deliberately, professionals will enjoy every part of the progress rather than hasten to a perfect future. By introducing pauses, breathing techniques, or reflection breaks between planning cycles, the clarity and the urge to control everything will be decreased. An example is a software designer who would look at her progress conscientiously at noon instead of continuously updating project outlines. These practices promote action and awareness.

Figure 3.4: Breaking Procrastination Cycles

Figure 3.4 above points out that proactive planning interferes with the process of procrastination. A meta-analysis study analyzed time-management training and planning interventions, which showed that these interventions significantly decrease procrastination and enhance task follow-through.

There is also over-planning on the team level. Collective perfectionism slows down projects in most workplaces since groups of people have to agree to a project before deciding to move on it. Rigby et al. (2018) stated that agile frameworks are the solution. Agile systems sub-divide large projects into brief, intensive sprints and subsequent reviews of feedback.

Every sprint focuses on knowledge and flexibility as opposed to perfection. The early prototypes are used in place of the exhaustive blueprints and promote early testing and accelerated innovation. The strategy minimizes stagnation and creates momentum by creating a continuous improvement.

The other method of preventing over-planning is by concentrating on execution-first learning. Professionals do not contemplate the possible issues; they start with a little experiment and develop it, depending on the feedback. Psychological safety promotes this kind of experimentation because it diminishes the fear of errors. Do-not-learn teams are quicker in innovating and their morale is higher. Purposeful planners and perfectionists differ in the desire to take action even when the future is unclear.

Balanced planning is also supported by emotional intelligence. Self-awareness and self-regulation help professionals to understand when planning is avoidance. Emotionally intelligent persons take time to enquire whether further planning is value adding or action postponing. They shift the emphasis to significant outcomes as opposed to procedural comfort. As an example, a marketing strategist who has developed a campaign schedule can see whether revisions enhance the message clarity or just allow the desire to control to pass.

Goal setting is also a part of purposeful planning. Perfectionists tend to underrate the unpredictability of life and work. Flexibility in scheduling enhances well-being by enabling people to deal with interruptions without feeling guilty. The professionals can secure their concentration by scheduling deep work and having open times to address any emergent requirements. Such a balance is what converts uncertainty into manageable variation, as opposed to stress.

Figure 3.5: Breaking Procrastination Cycles

Figure 3.5 above demonstrates the traditional cue-routine-reward system of the formation of behavioral habits. Behavioral psychology indicates that the reinforcement of routine habits has the power to reinforce good work practices and stable behavior in the long run.

Lastly, the cultural context of planning has an effect on behavior. Over preparation is valued as hard work in some places of work. However, in Indian universities, when the new system of assessment was moved at the cost of the number of hours spent to the number of results, the wastage planning was reduced and this enhanced the overall efficiency. Flexibility and punctuality can be rewarded by managers to help in goal-oriented planning rather than comprehensive planning.

3.3 True-to-Life Scenario

Rania and Miguel are now two analysts who had worked in one of the multinational companies in Madrid in the dynamic world of corporate finance. They were qualified and also determined and yet they differed in their approach to planning. Rania was a picture of deliberate plans, and Miguel an example of over planning. Their experience demonstrates that there are a number of planning habits that impact performance, well-being, and growth.

Rania started every week by choosing three main goals: complete the analysis of the quarter, create the slide deck to present at the next board meeting, and mentor a junior colleague. As Aeon et al. (2021) note, prioritizing a few clear things is better to control, balance emotions, and reduce anxiety. Rania set aside blocks of time on each task and created buffer time in the event of unforeseen problems. Her strategist was plain and straightforward; not ornamental. She focused her efforts on analysis and insight instead of format and details.

The plan of Miguel seemed to be very detailed and it became counterproductive. He started Monday by creating a complicated color-coded timetable with each half-hour broken down into micro-tasks. He developed several spreadsheets to follow subtasks and then edited them many times to achieve the visual perfection.

By Tuesday afternoon, his planning was taking more time than his work. The over-organization of pre-task processes is associated with less task accomplishment and increased stress. The quest to achieve perfect organization consumed the mental power of Miguel even before implementation started.

Upon the presentation of Wednesday, Rania presented a succinct data-driven analysis that was direct to the concern of management. The executive team was impressed by her clarity and liked her accuracy and flexibility. The slides made by Miguel were visually perfect but not deep. His excessive emphasis on design did not leave much time to analyze.

Consequently, he had difficulties with responding to follow-up questions. When a person is engaged in something, such as Rania, this state is known as flow, which is created by the optimal combination of challenge and skill. Flow is created when attention is paid to doing something meaningful instead of pretending to be in control.

The results were not only performance based but also affected emotional health. Rania claimed that she felt confident, calm, and organized during the week. On the contrary, Miguel was stressed and unhappy in spite of his working long hours.

Emotional regulation is enhanced when one views his or her plans as flexible and adaptive rather than fixed. Intentional planners like Rania have recovery time in their timetables, which gives their energy a chance to revive throughout the week. Her walks and coffee breaks in the afternoon were conscious breaks that kept the mind focused and creative.

A survey on productivity and well-being was carried out in the human-resources department of the firm several months later. The outcomes were the manifestation of purposeful and over-planned behavior. Employees who had a balanced structure and adaptability had increased engagement, work-life integration, and a reduced number of burnout symptoms. The perfectionism organizational cost was reflected in Miguel being very meticulous but rigid in planning; his results were delayed, he was more fatigued and less innovative.

The approach of Rania slowly affected her work mates. She also launched five-minute morning stand-ups, where the team members were asked to give their one priority that they had to get done in the day. This practice substituted protracted status meetings and confusion on duties. Bakker and Demerouti (2017) state that shared planning improves engagement and increases alignment in teams. In a quarter, the department headed by Rania decreased the overtime by 18 percent and reported an increase in job satisfaction.

Miguel later looked back at his plights. He understood that he was over-planning because he was afraid of making mistakes and that he was afraid of looking unprepared. Dweck (2016) argues that people who hold a growth mindset, which assumes that individuals can improve their skills through effort, perceive imperfection as a learning opportunity.

The calmness of Rania gave him the confidence to experiment with shorter and simpler plans. He started to set himself only three tasks that he had to complete daily, based on a model that resembles hers. Gradually, his productivity was increased, his stress was reduced, and he found pleasure in his job.

The management of the company understood the influence of Rania and provided her with the post of cross-departmental project leader. The model of the training of the firm to new managers included the strategy she employed, which is defining priorities, flexibility on planning, and decisiveness. Meanwhile, it was demonstrated by the metamorphosis of Miguel that even long-term over-planners may be brought to be efficient once more by a change of attitude. The two began sharing junior employees together and it was she who was planning everything and he was the one who was detailed.

The overall lessons are reflected in their story. To begin with, deliberate planning values utility, as opposed to excellence. The plans are there so as to spearhead the decisions and not to stifle creativity. According to Grant and Parker (2009), adaptive planning enables the establishment of resilience and the encouragement of lifelong learning.

Secondly, over-planning reduces spontaneity. People concentrate on polishing plans as opposed to executing them and this slows down progress and increases stress. Thirdly, true efficiency is the acceptance of uncertainty. There is no strategy that can foresee all the variables; hence, winning is determined by flexibility and responsiveness.

These lessons cut across the professions. Adaptive planning is useful to engineers in Dubai who have to plan the logistics of the site, educators in Toronto who have to design hybrid lessons, and healthcare workers in Manila who have to coordinate the shifts. In all the situations, efficiency will increase where structure is matched with flexibility. A plan which develops with new information is better than the plan which is not adaptable.

Intentional strategists such as Rania know that development is cyclical. They start when things are not ideal, receive feedback and continually change. Over planners such as Miguel tend to wait until the perfect conditions come (which never come). Plans only become good intentions unless they instantly transform into hard work. The approach of Rania was such that it was planning to her action and not vice versa.

The larger connotation is both psychological and professional. Stoeber and Otto (2006) indicate that perfectionism fulfills short-term control, but destroys long-term motivation. Intentional planning, in its turn, strikes a balance between control and flexibility. It turns planning into an offensive process rather than a defensive behavior. It liberates the mind to be innovative and collaborate.

Gradually, the lesson was finished with the transformation of Miguel. In a seminar held internally, when questioned about his change, he responded: "I understood that it is not to plan but to do wisely." His commentary was the spirit of intentional planning, an attitude that cherishes momentum, flexibility, and education in itself rather than accuracy.

Purposeful strategists achieve this due to their willingness to be uncertain rather than resist uncertainty. Their time-tables are guides, not fences. They understand that the real worth of a plan is its ability to conform to reality. The opposition between Rania and Miguel in any profession and culture is a universal decision: to prepare and prepare indefinitely or to start, to adapt and to finish. The distinction between them is not in the intelligence or in the effort, but in the intention.

3.4 Practical Planning Tips

Intentionality is based on focus, order, and moderation. Covey (2020) posits that when people organize their week according to their values, they become efficient and peaceful. Practical planning is not the complicated tools or color-coded schedules; it is about the habits that are developed based on the evidence-based practices. The principles below provide practical solutions on how to make planning an action.

3.4.1. Begin with the End in Mind

The vision of success in planning should always begin with a clear vision. Freund and Hennecke (2015) state that backward planning, which involves identifying the desired result and tracing steps backwards, establishes logical framework and trust.

By visualizing the final goal, the professionals will recognize the milestones that should be achieved and remove distractions. As an example, a project coordinator who is planning an event can start with the target date and work backward to book the venue, do marketing and logistics. This will avoid the last minute rush and every action will be made to add up to the overall objective.

3.4.2. Use SMART Goals

SMART goals, which consist of Specific, Measurable, Achievable, Relevant, and Time-bound, change the abstract dreams into practical goals. Plans are transformed into scheduled commitments by combining SMART goals and time-blocking. An obvious example is a teacher who wants to complete grading 50 papers in days. Breaking the task down into quantifiable tasks like ten papers a day enhances accountability and minimizes procrastination.

3.4.3. Limit Task Lists

Clear (2018) states that long to-do lists tend to consume attention and cause decision fatigue. Setting the goal of three main tasks per day helps to focus more. Those professionals who accomplish these high-impact tasks initially generate momentum which will be carried into the day. This strategy is based on the idea that it is the quality of focus rather than the quantity of work.

3.4.4. Integrate Reflection Time

The improvement requires weekly reflection. Aeon et al. (2021) argue that professionals who plan time to reflect are more likely to be clear and reduce stress. The need to pause and look at progress will assist in identifying what has been successful, what has not succeeded and what needs to be changed. This self-evaluation makes planning a learning process. The review at the end of the week, for example, a list of three achievements and one improvement point, keeps the planner focused and flexible.

3.4.5. Flexibility and Structure of Balance

Very inflexible plans fail in most cases when the conditions alter. Flexible scheduling positively affects the productivity and well-being of employees who experience uncertainty. This can be done through the establishment of buffer slots in the calendar of professionals. As an example, a one-hour gap between the meetings will provide an opportunity to have an emergency or time to focus on the work. Flexibility will make sure that planning does not limit creativity.

3.4.6. Utilize Visual Aids

Visual organization enhances the memory and motivation. Visual boards or Gantt charts as reported by Mazmanian et al. (2013) enhance task ownership and decrease mental clutter. An example is a marketing team that can observe the stages in a campaign on a common Kanban board where members can look at progress and deadlines without going through the board. The perception of improvement creates the sense of responsibility and improves cooperation.

3.4.7. Valuing Rest and Recovery is a Priority

Effective planners know that productivity is not time but rather energy. Sonnentag (2018) mentions that recovery periods help to regain focus and avoid burnout. Rest is therefore a planned activity. Practitioners that take brief pauses or daily silent hours maintain long-term performance. A refreshed mind can work with information more quickly, and make quality decisions, which at the end leads to high performance.

3.4.8. Share and Discuss Strategies

Bakker and Demerouti (2017) claim that the transparency of planning increases team engagement and coordination. By sharing schedules, people will avoid redundancy and be held accountable to one another. Contemporary team-working technologies like shared-calendars and online dashboards can coordinate organizational action. Even a morning check-in, when every team member sets one key goal, harmonizes the attention of the group.

3.4.9. Review and Recalibrate

Plans have to adapt to the changing situations. Grant and Parker (2009) underlined the importance of adaptive planning as the means of enhancing resilience and building ongoing improvements. Reviews weekly assist professionals to assess the outcomes and revise the goals. Taking every week as a new beginning, people have momentum and do not feel overwhelmed. Review flexibility helps to avoid frustration when the plans are faced with unforeseen challenges.

3.4.10. Celebrate Progress

It is important to celebrate small wins to be motivated. Amabile and Kramer (2011) note that the perception of progress on a daily basis increases satisfaction and strengthens positive behavior. Intentional strategists recognize milestones, however small. As an illustration, a personal reward or even a short team acknowledgement can be used to complete a report earlier than expected. Productivity is converted into pleasure through positive reinforcement.

The tips are illustrated by a civil engineer in Johannesburg. Being in charge of several construction sites, he starts each week by defining three significant objectives. He employs backward planning to plan every milestone and has some flexible slots in case of weather disruptions. His team provides feedback on the progress via visual dashboard and reports outcomes via brief weekly reflection. Using these steps, the team is always able to meet deadlines with minimal overtime and increased morale.

Purpose planning is neither about perfection nor direction, it is about direction. When people plan their days, they substitute disorder with order. Covey (2020) explains that when people proactively plan according to their principles, then planning an ordinary work becomes a significant step forward.

Professionals regain control over their time and energy by establishing SMART goals, reducing the number of tasks per day, balancing between structure and flexibility, and identifying progress. Intentional planning helps them to change in the time of need, be centered on what is really important, and be successful in the long run in personal and professional life.

3.5 Chapter Summary

Meaningful productivity is based on purposeful planning. Success starts when people have certain, quantifiable objectives and make them part of their day-to-day routine. Intentional planning is about clarity, flexibility, and simplicity as opposed to perfection. According to Gollwitzer and Sheeran (2006), clear implementation intentions which are the connection between intention and behavior can be used to turn motivation into uninterrupted progress.

In this chapter, a number of methods were highlighted: backward planning, time-blocking, and SMART goal-setting. The principle of prioritizing the big rocks by Covey (2020) promotes the high-value tasks that should be done first. Equally, Freund and Hennecke (2015) indicated that time-blocking helps avoid distractions of attention, whereas backward design helps avoid last-minute stress.

It is also important not to overplan and be perfectionists. Stoeber and Otto (2006) warned that perfectionism reduces productivity and creates anxiety. Rather, the adoption of the rule of good enough and conscious flexibility result in improvement. Examples of cases in Madrid, Kuala Lumpur and Johannesburg demonstrated the way in which intentional planning can support performance and well-being in any profession and culture.

Key Takeaways

- Purposeful planning transforms the vision into some form of action.
- Adaptability meaning increases resilience and innovativeness.
- SMART goals are a guide on visible advancement.
- Too much focus on planning is a waste: simplicity gains momentum.
- Reflection connects the progress to the growth of an individual.

Embrace the Following this Week

1. Write 3 SMART goals and set time on each of them.
2. Use the rule of good enough in one task and complete it in time.
3. On your week shear one slot on reflections.
4. Tell a colleague about your plan with him or her to hold yourself responsible.
5. Rewarding a single minor achievement at the end of each week goes a long way in strengthening the process.

Chapter 4: Hack 3: Streamline Your Workflow

All professionals, be it a teacher in Toronto, a designer in Nairobi or an operations' lead in Dubai, will get to the same point at some point: there are too many things that demand too little time. With the increase in responsibilities, processes get entangled, and energy disperses. Complex systems squander human potential by entombing creativity in unnecessary processes. Streamlining is an art of learning how to make work flow. It involves developing processes that are transparent, effective and reproducible without consuming time and attention.

Streamlining does not mean working faster, but working smoother. When the tasks are interrelated, then productivity will be natural and not imposed. A study conducted by Hughes et al. (2025) revealed that professionals who optimize their workflows on a regular basis have their performance and well-being increased by 30 percent. This chapter aims at demonstrating that anyone, irrespective of industry, can simplify, delegate, and automate effectively. Using the concepts of Lean Six Sigma to daily operations, you can create systems that are time-saving and result multipliers.

Figure 4.1: Less is More

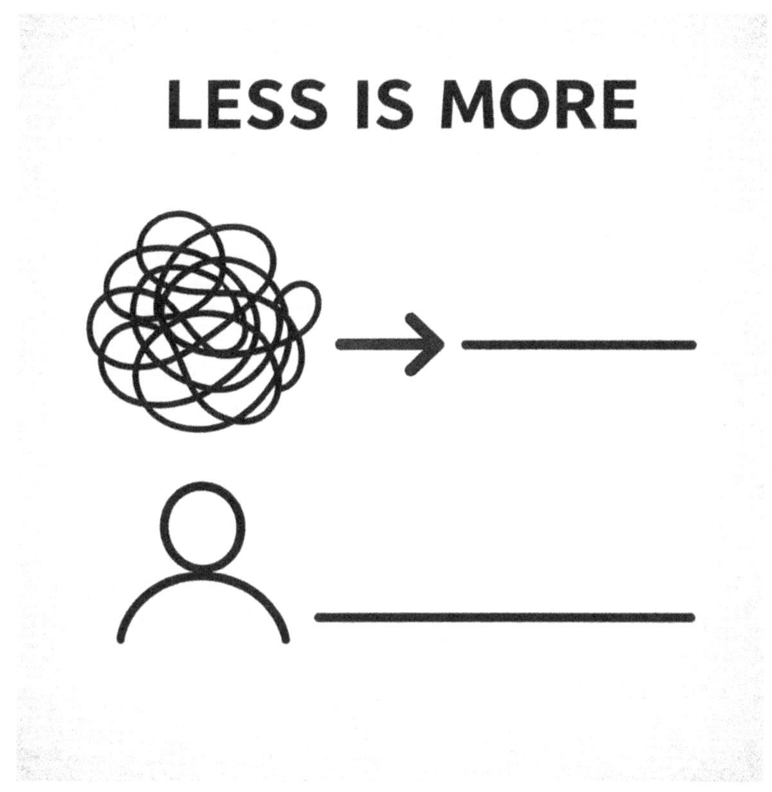

Figure 4.1 above is an example of a shift between disorder and order, a messy desk turning into a clean, concentrated one. It represents the elimination of unnecessary activities and distractions to increase clarity. Simplicity is not dependent on doing less but doing more with purposefulness, balance, and a sense of purpose, as highlighted in the visual.

4.1 Simplifying Tasks and Processes

The initial step to streamlining is simplification. The majority of inefficiency is not caused by people but by the processes that they follow. Making things and processes simpler is concerned with defining what is really valuable and eliminating all that is not.

Complexity usually disguises itself as professionalism, yet the true mastery is in clarity.

4.1.1 Identify Friction Points

The initial process improvement step is to identify the points of friction. Friction is manifested when the effort does not yield progress. Drawing a map of your daily workflow will show you the steps that are not necessary to accelerate the momentum. An example is that a marketing analyst in Cape Town noticed that she was taking hours to reformat weekly reports. She created a standard template and halved the process time and minimized stress.

Figure 4.2: Multiply Your Impact

The picture in Figure 4.2 above shows overlapping gears or swelling nodes, which is the way that structured processes contribute to outcomes. It is a visual representation of the power of smart planning, delegation, and teamwork- it demonstrates that strategic coordination can lead to results that are larger than those that can be achieved by a single person. Efficiency does not consist of the effort multiplied but of the direction multiplied.

4.1.2 Apply the 80/20 Principle

The Pareto principle is a lesson that 20 percent of the work can produce 80 percent of the outcomes. Koch (2011) argues that performance can be changed by identifying those few actions that are vital. The questions that professionals should ask on a regular basis are: What activities produce the most valuable results? What activities produce noise without value? By targeting the high impact 20 percent, you liberate resources to innovation and profound work.

4.1.3 Reduce Decision Fatigue

Too much minor decision-making is a drain on the mind. Low-value decisions made repeatedly lower the concentration and strength of will. These micro-decisions can be reduced by routines and automation with the aid of simplification. An example is that an engineer in Singapore automates daily reporting and reserves deep work hours of no-meeting. Every decision that is eliminated is time saved.

4.1.4 Normalize Repetitive Processes

Quality is constructed by repetition in standardization. The developer of the Toyota Production System, Ohno (2019) stressed that regular processes eliminate rework and mistakes. Templates and checklists can also be used in personal productivity. A university lecturer in Kuala Lumpur is able to save time by using ready-made lesson plans. The standardization of recurring processes enables the professionals to be creative rather than repetitive.

4.1.5 Work of Sequence and Batch

The inability to concentrate is caused by switching between irrelevant tasks. Research reveals that task-switching may reduce productivity by up to 40 percent. Cognitive load is lowered by combining similar tasks (responding to emails or checking off reports). Backtracking is also reduced by sequencing tasks. When the routine activities are running in unison, the mental energy is not used in solving the complex problems.

Figure 4.3: Equip for Efficiency

The visual in figure 4.3 above shows a clean workspace and a well-organized digital tools, computers, notebooks, dashboards, and so on. It is a symbol of preparation, structure and readiness as the pillars of productivity. The figure conveys the idea that the availability of the appropriate tools and systems makes the workflow easier and helps to maintain the same level of performance in the tasks and environments.

4.1.6 Manage Digital Clutter

Productivity is silently undermined by digital disorganization. Notifications and open tabs are distracting and cause stress. Research states that multitasking between devices decreases accuracy and memory. Reduce the number of applications in your online life by having a single reliable task manager, disabling notifications and screen time limits.

4.1.7 Consider and Revise on a Continuing Basis

Simplification is a continuous process. This is Kaizen, or continuous improvement. Periodically audit workflows and inquire: What can we do away with, automate or delegate? The process of improvement does not occur accidentally, but it develops out of curiosity and regularity. Minor alterations, repeated many times, have exponential outcomes.

4.1.8 Eradicate, Mechanize, Outsource

The simplification philosophy is based on a single mantra: Get rid of what wastes time, automate what is repeated, and delegate what can be done better by others. Perez (2014) states that emotional intelligence enables professionals to understand when to give up. People are often unable to streamline because of the need to control. Releasing minor tasks will allow one to think strategically.

Figure 4.4: Eliminate, Automate, Delegate

Figure 4.4 above shows three levels of production activities, which are eliminating unnecessary work, automating repetitive work, and sharing common responsibilities. It expresses the spirit of lean efficiency: simplicity in prioritization. The figure is a visual representation of the main message of the chapter that intentional systems enable professionals to concentrate on what is really valuable.

Streamlining operations creates transparency, uniformity and trust. As systems get lighter, decision-making becomes better and stress levels reduce. Aeon et al. (2021) observed that practitioners who streamline their processes are more satisfied and less burned. They save time and energy by eliminating the needless complexity to get back to the work which is important.

The following section examines the relationship between simplification and collaboration: how the ability to delegate and outsource can be used to bring efficiency to the team, as well as the individual.

4.2 Mastering Delegation and Outsourcing

Delegation does not mean to give work to others; it is empowering to collaborate. Perez (2014) states that when professionals understand that success is multiplied by shared responsibility, then they are truly efficient in leadership. Most individuals are afraid of delegating due to the fear of losing control or poor performance. However, Drucker (2006) reveals that no leader can do great work by himself. The trick is in clear, trustful, and feedback delegation.

4.2.1 The Change of Mindset: The Attitude of Control to Cooperation

Intentional delegation starts with trust. Control is usually synonymous with quality, yet micromanagement is energy-consuming and creativity-destroying. Dweck (2006) argues that a growth mindset allows leaders to view the learning curve of others as a part of the progress and not a threat to efficiency. When delegation is a coaching experience and not a test, teams become stronger and more independent.

The above was experienced by an operations supervisor in Dubai. Overwhelmed with several client projects, he began delegating research and documentation to his staff. He was initially worried about quality and came up with a simple review checklist and brief feedback meetings. In less than a month, the quality of output increased, and turnaround time reduced by a quarter. When delegated, it is not a burden but a multiplier.

4.2.2 The Currency of Delegation is Clarity

Delegation does not work when instructions are not clear. Research by Amabile and Kramer (2011) shows that employees are most engaged when they know the reason why they are doing something. Purpose should be articulated just like expectations. Any delegated task must respond to three questions: What needs to be done? Why is it important? When is it due? The confusion is avoided by a simple shared document with deadlines, desired outcomes, and metrics.

To illustrate the above, a digital content team in Johannesburg has a common Kanban board to control the assigned tasks. The task cards have objectives, steps and status updates. Such openness promotes responsibility and independence.

4.2.3 Match Roles to Strengths

Delegation flourishes when it is in line with personal competencies. Individuals perform best when they are doing what they are good at and not what they are bad at. A leader with the knowledge of the capabilities of his team is able to delegate tasks in a strategic manner. As a reference, a team member who is fond of writing can write reports, and a team member who has visual design capabilities can prepare presentations. Delegation of work to talents improves performance and morale.

To achieve this, practitioners can either apply short term team tests or keep a list of skills inventory. According to Belbin (2012), the various roles, including thinkers, implementers, and coordinators are uniquely important in success, in addition to the fact that they play different roles.

4.2.4 Develop Accountability Systems

Accountability-free delegation is anarchy. Accountability is not control- it is transparency of results. Grant and Parker (2009) state that teams work more effectively when the responsibility is well-established and the performance is assessed on a regular basis. It is good to establish milestones and feedback to keep tasks delegated on track. Check-ins every week are better than daily interruptions, which provide room to do things independently.

4.2.5 Outsource Strategically

Outsourcing goes beyond in-house teams. Modern professionals have the advantage of outsourcing administrative or technical tasks that do not focus on the main objectives. Time-intensive activities can be addressed effectively by freelancers, virtual assistants and specialized agencies. An example is a consultant in Singapore who outsources the invoicing of clients and scheduling on social media so that he can concentrate more on strategy and coaching.

Nonetheless, effective outsourcing requires accurate expectations. Write a clear scope, deliverables outline and make use of the project management tools to communicate. Outsourcing is organized and quantified with the help of digital collaboration tools like Asana or Notion.

4.2.6 Delegation Emotional Intelligence

Delegation needs both the form and feeling. Boyatzis et al. (2000) state that emotionally intelligent leaders express gratitude, are active listeners, and acknowledge efforts. Motivation is maintained by simple gestures, such as a thank you note to a colleague who has put in effort or the recognition of creativity. Teams work well when they are trusted and valued.

Emotional intelligence is also useful in enabling leaders to delegate emotionally challenging tasks like feedback or conflict management. Leaders are able to uphold respect by being open and fair even during difficult times.

4.2.7 The Feedback Loop

Feedback is the end, not the start of effective delegation. Learning takes place when people think about the results and find the ways to improve them. A positive review process turns delegation into a skill development process. It makes sure that the current project is smoother than the previous one.

4.2.8 Breaking the Delegation Barriers

The fear of losing control, fear of inefficiency, or fear of dependency are some of the reasons why many professionals do not delegate. Studies reveal that this resistance is usually fueled by perfectionism. To overcome it, it is necessary to redefine delegation as shared leadership. Intentional leaders view delegation as an alliance of direction and confidence.

Anxiety is reduced by developing documentation systems like checklists and progress trackers. Confidence supersedes hesitation when there is structure. As Drucker (2006) observed, leaders are effective when they aim at contribution rather than control.

4.2.9 Delegation as Empowerment

Delegation gives power to both the sender and the receiver. When leaders delegate ownership in a prudent manner, others become initiative and self-directed. The sum of individual capacity of a team increases with time. Dweck (2006) posits that empowerment fosters a culture of growth, in which learning and innovation flourish.

One of the design managers in Nairobi once remarked that when she stopped doing everything herself, the team began to surprise her. Delegation enabled her to be a strategic leader and not a reactive leader. Modern efficiency is characterized by empowerment, rather than micromanagement.

Delegation is one of the major productivity multipliers when done deliberately. It is the conversion of individual effort into group intelligence. The following section discusses how technology and automation can apply this principle, which is to make work not only faster but smarter.

4.3 Leveraging Technology for Efficiency

Technology has been made to be dependent on the modern productivity. The issue, however, lies in the fact that one has access to digital tools, but knows how to use them purposefully. The majority of professionals adopt technology in a haphazard manner and therefore more disruption than productivity is achieved. Technology of productivity is not expected to take the place of human focus but it should be an extension of it. The digital efficiency is not tied to working out the clock but working efficiently.

Contemporary practitioners are in an environment where machines are offering speed and precision. However, the actual benefit is deliberate integration. The selection of tools that fit certain workflows may decrease redundant work, ease communication, and avoid mental overload.

Research conducted by Hughes et al. (2025) indicate that structured technology adoption helped organizations that trained their teams on workflow automation to improve performance by 30 percent. Digital dashboards, shared task managers, and automated reports are tools that can be used to release valuable cognitive space to creativity and decision-making.

Figure 4.5: Automate the Mundane

Figure 4.5 above shows that there are routine tasks like reporting or scheduling, which are carried out by robotic systems or other digital tools. It is a symbol of the power of automation in order to reduce the human error, the free time, and the focus to the creative or analytical work. The figure argues in favor of the fact that technology cannot and should not replace human capability.

This change is an indispensable aspect of automation. Even the regular activities, such as scheduling meetings, sending notifications or making weekly reports can be easily delegated to software. Such computerized systems eliminate duplication and give uniformity. Seryapina (2018) states that automation enhances goal attainment through the reduction of human error and mental fatigue.

The above can be illustrated by the fact that a marketing coordinator in Kuala Lumpur used automated campaign reporting templates. A process that required six hours was reduced to an hour. Using technology in a wise way does not dehumanize work, it restores focus to the things that are important.

But technology can be excessive as well. Digital fatigue as a phenomenon has been a tacit barrier to focus. It has been found out that the constant notifications diminish task accuracy and attention. The solution is the digital minimalism, which is to possess fewer tools, but to use them more.

It is recommended that professionals audit their apps and platforms regularly and only keep those that contribute to their attaining their core purposes. To use a more concrete example, instead of multiple messaging apps, a small business team can rely on one combined solution, such as Slack or Microsoft Teams. It must never be concerned about the quantity but clarity.

Digital integration also enhances collaboration. The sharing of tasks, resources, and updates is more open and fluid in terms of teamwork. Tools such as Trello, Notion, or Asana allow the professionals to observe the progress and identify the bottlenecks early in the game.

Belbin (2012) state that team synergy is enhanced by clarity of shared goals. Online teamwork tools have substituted disorganized email communications with organized work processes that foster responsibility. In this regard, technology is the linking factor that brings people together to form one system.

Nevertheless, digital efficiency does not depend on tools but habits. Technology does not make people productive; it only magnifies the actions it reinforces. An untidy employee will remain untidy with new software. The use of technology should be purposeful, which means that it must be disciplined, with limits on screen time, priorities in tasks, and breaks without devices. Professionals ought to create digital hygiene by sorting out cluttered files, turning off the unnecessary notifications, and saving time to engage in deep work.

The use of artificial intelligence in workflow optimization is increasingly becoming a reality. Huang and Rust (2021) state that AI-based systems help professionals to make better decisions by forecasting and giving automatic suggestions. AI scheduling systems may propose the most appropriate time to hold a meeting based on the calendar data, and AI-based writing assistants may help to make the text more readable and accurate.

These innovations save on administration and enhance concentration on strategic thinking. As an example, a design consultant in Dubai incorporates AI analytics to detect trends in clients, which saves him or her hours of manual data analysis every week.

Although it promises, AI should be applied ethically. Judging and creativity can be undermined through overreliance. Intentional application implies human intuition and machine accuracy. The most successful professionals are the ones who do not work on technology but with it. Human expertise should not be substituted by automation.

Digital efficiency is also dependent on security and privacy. The simplification of systems must not be done at the expense of data integrity. One must use reliable software, enable encryptions, and perform frequent data backups. Lean Six Sigma concept of error-proofing is also applicable to digital processes. It is always more effective to prevent than to cure.

In order to balance human and digital performance, the principle of tech harmony can be applied. This is a notion that Hughes et al. (2025) proposes, which implies that each tool must have a purpose, fit into a routine, and minimize, rather than add to mental load. A middle ground will make technology enhance human creativity rather than stifle it.

This is well depicted in the story of a Nairobi-based architect. He dealt with several client projects and frequently encountered problems with communication delays and document mess. He implemented a cloud-based project management system, which provided a common workspace between clients and employees.

Automatic synchronization of drawings, revisions, and budgets was done. In two months, the missed deadlines reduced by half. More to the point, he recovered evenings to rest. Technology made not only his work easier, but also his life.

Finally, the best thing about technology is that it renders systems invisible. The smooth operation of workflow leads to a natural flow of energy between activities with no resistance. The tools are pushed to the background, and human creativity is in the limelight. When technology is used in a purposeful manner, professionals who are open to digital simplicity find that technology is a silent accomplice. It transforms the complicated into the clear and the movement into the development.

The following part expands on these concepts by discussing the way the Lean Six Sigma mindset, which was initially applied in manufacturing, can be applied to personal productivity. Such an attitude assists people in creating their daily systems in a very accurate manner, removing waste and maximizing value at each point.

4.4 True-to-Life Scenario: Delegation and Automation in Action

A young operations manager called Layla was in charge of a growing team in a logistics company in the center of the busy startup scene in Dubai. Hundreds of emails, spreadsheets, and customer requests were the order of the day. Her work was great, and her dedication was great, but her work was too much.

She thought that good leaders were supposed to be omnipresent and omnipotent. The result was exhaustion. This perfection-based behavior frequently results in burnout as it restricts delegation and causes a continuous feeling of pressure to do everything perfectly.

First of all, Layla tried to cope with it by working more hours. Late into the night she slept and responded to the messages and manually recorded the progress. The more she worked the greater were her mistakes. Delays were experienced in reporting systems, delayed customer response was drawn and her department used to have her make all decisions. However, she appeared to be extremely productive at the cost of mental clarity and belief in the team.

All this came to pass when one of her senior mentors indicated that she could take the two step approach: to delegate those tasks that required human attention and automate those that did not. It was an effective but simple change. Layla started by listing all her weekly tasks, which included making follow-ups with clients, updating the suppliers, reporting on data, and scheduling. She then divided them into three, eliminate, automate and delegate.

Her initial experiment was on automation. She did not have to send daily progress reports manually but through an automated spreadsheet that was linked to the internal system of the company. The information was updated on an hourly basis and gave her team real time visibility. This one change saved her two hours per day.

She subsequently incorporated a project management application which coordinated work, time frames, and remarks within a single computerized platform. Hughes et al. (2025) notes that these automation systems enhance the accuracy of decisions and decrease the communication delays by up to 35 percent.

Delegation came next. Layla began training her team heads to manage some of the client segments. She was slow to start with and she came up with a clear structure that had an objective, weekly meetings and free communication. Several weeks later she could see that something had changed: her team became more creative. They offered new patterns of delivery that were no longer under her control which reduced delays of transport by 12 percent. Layla was not doing strategic planning but firefighting.

Layla had emotional issues as well. She was habitually accused of leaving work that she had done on her own. However, Dweck (2006) affirm that leaders develop in cases where they embrace their weaknesses and when the leaders also enable others to learn. Layla embraced this mindset. She complimented small successes, commended hard labor and gave supportive feedback. Trust replaced tension. The crew had already begun to deliver projects before time.

Technology was her friend and not her slave. Robotized reminders, analytics boards, and AI-based scheduling software managed what previously consumed her time. She was using the Lean approach to make her decisions, as she would remove any task that did not add value to the customers or the team. What was left was good work that motivated development.

By the end of a quarter, the department managed by Layla finished its work 18 percent faster and was more satisfied. Her evenings were now no longer spent on emails. Her leadership became even stronger due to delegating and automation, rather than weakening it. It was an experience that productivity does not imply working harder but development of systems that work to your favor.

Her story is an echo of a greater truth: it is easy to be successful and succeed on trust. Intelligent delegation and efficient automation of professionals does not only do more, but also promotes development in others. The case of Layla is a case where chaos was turned into harmony by use of technology, structure, and emotional intelligence.

4.5 Lean Six Sigma Mindset for Personal Productivity

The Lean Six Sigma mentality, which was previously the preserve of manufacturing, has now been adopted as a philosophy of the contemporary professional who wants to achieve personal efficiency. It is all about one thing, which is to maximize value and minimize waste. Efficiency starts when people recognize the effort that is not needed and substitute it with meaningful action. When used at the individual level, Lean Six Sigma changes the disorderly routines into elegant systems of enhancement.

Figure 4.6: Process Makes Perfect

The diagram in Figure 4.6 above shows a continuous improvement loop- commonly referred to as Plan, Do, Check and Act. It embodies the Lean six sigma concept of Kaizen: continuous improvement by learning. The picture repeats the fact that mastery is a journey and never a destination and it is a process of constant review, constant feedback, constant minor corrections that are disciplined.

Lean Six Sigma philosophy is premised on five concepts, which are define, measure, analyze, improve and control (DMAIC). These steps help individuals in designing the work processes that can be measured in terms of outcomes. To provide an example, a student will be in a position to define the aim of writing a research paper, review the progress on a daily basis, review difficulties, revise strategies depending on the reaction, and control distractions through time-blocking. Business, Acadia or personal projects can be done under the same model.

George (2006) states that effective professionals consider productivity a living system- one that is constantly assessed and optimized. Continuous improvement or Kaizen is not a revolution but an evolution. Minor improvements made day by day build up to miraculous outcomes. Such an attitude promotes inquisitiveness and toughness. Purposeful planners do not respond to issues but explore their causes and re-engineer their approaches.

Another aspect of lean thinking is the removal of waste that is not only limited to materials but also time, attention, and energy. The seven wastes that are found in the Six Sigma, which include defects, overproduction, waiting, untapped talent, transport, inventory, and motion, are also present in personal work. Spending too much time checking emails, holding unnecessary meetings or multitasking among unrelated activities are all wastes. Ohno (2019) argues that excellence starts with people eliminating what does not add value to the creation of value.

Two habits can be applied by professionals in order to implement the Lean principles. Start with defining of value: what is important today? Measure success by quantitative measurements such as goals achievement or vitality. Assess the routines on a weekly basis to determine inefficiencies. It is good trying out new methods, including substituting multitasking with single-task attention. Finally, control the process by designing discipline-reviewing plans, reflection, and process improvement.

Technology is useful in this cycle provided that it is applied in a prudent way. Digital dashboards and time trackers and automation tools are used to measure and visualize improvement. Though, technology can only enhance Lean systems in case it is human purpose-driven. Even the most desirable systems produce clutters by default.

Minimizing variation is another important aspect of Six Sigma thinking. Unstable work patterns result in unstable outcome. Setting of standard procedures, e.g., morning planning routine or weekly reflection stabilizes performance. Consistency makes it possible to predict, and this predictability helps in creativity. When processes are running well, there is more room in the mind to be innovative.

Lean productivity also focuses on emotional balance. Internal noise that hinders focus is over-planning, perfectionism, and digital clutter. Perez (2014) state that emotional regulation enhances the quality of attention. The introduction of mindfulness or short moments of reflection into everyday work makes the Lean philosophy consistent with psychological well-being.

A civil engineer in Johannesburg puts this attitude into practice. His firm adopted Lean in order to streamline project management. He began to apply the same principles in his own life, set clear goals, examine data on performance and make his morning routine. With time, he understood that the fewer decisions made the better the outcomes. His projects were completed earlier than anticipated and his employees were less pressurized. He knew that Lean Six Sigma was not a business model, but a philosophy of life.

The Lean Six Sigma culture inculcates the notion of dynamism on productivity. It is a living breathing, adaptive, dynamic system, which advances through being conscious and perfected. Mindfulness and structure when combined will help professionals develop resilience and clarity. Swiftness has ceased to be productivity, it is idleness in motion.

4.6 Chapter Summary

Streamlining work entails creating systems that are purposeful and not pressurizing. Making things easier makes the mind to be less cluttered, delegation makes an individual more capable, and technology improves flow when applied with purpose. Every concept of efficiency, including automation, Lean Six Sigma, and others, reminds professionals that productivity starts with clarity. The research and stories in this chapter show one thing, that meaningful work is never about doing more but doing what matters better.

Delegation fosters trust and development, automation saves time, and Lean principles optimize performance by continually improving it. The most effective professionals are not the ones who hurry but those who think, plan and adapt. The balance between human judgment and digital accuracy will determine the success of further development of the modern work. Workflow optimization consists of recovering time and developing structures that facilitate your values, aspirations, and vitality. It is not simplicity to which ambition is opposed, but its foundation.

Key Takeaways

- Intentional planning makes the vision some kind of action.
- One that refers to adaptability makes him/herself more resilient and innovative.
- SMART goals are a roadmap on perceptible progress.
- Excessive attention to planning is a waste; simplicity is on the offensive.
- Progress relates to the development of an individual in reflection.

This Week's Work

1. Write 3 SMART goals and allocate time to each one of them.
2. Apply the rule of "good enough on one thing" and deliver within time.
3. On your reflections: one slot on perceiving.
4. Share with a colleague and disclose to him or her your intention of holding yourself responsible.
5. The rewarding of a few small accomplishments at the close of every week is a long way in reinforcing the process.

Chapter 5: Hack 4- Harness the Power of Focus

Any major accomplishment starts with concentration. In a world where there are no limits to distractions, the skill of focusing attention has been one of the most useful human skills. Perez (2014) argues that attention is the secret of excellence since it dictates what the mind sees, thinks, and focuses on. However, contemporary work culture tends to confuse movement with development, and it rewards being busy instead of being clear. Professionals scroll their feeds, manage multiple meetings simultaneously, and work on multiple devices, losing what helps them remain creative and precise: attention.

Focus is not merely a question of concentration; it is the art of becoming disciplined in selecting a single thought, single goal or a single task out of the noise. According to Posner and Rothbart (1998), attention is a spotlight, as it illuminates what is important and shadows what is not. The following sections consider how to take that attention, de-junk cognitive space, and conserve cognitive energy and try to re-train the mind in the distracted world to think deeply again. Focus does not entail perfection but practice. Once professionals are taught to maintain attention, they recover their time, energy, and the possibility of doing meaningful and lasting work.

5.1 The Spotlight of Attention: How Focus Works

The power to focus is a silent power that is present in every human mind. Even complicated tasks are clear when the attention is constant. When it is shaky, work is multiplied, but gains lost. Posner and Rothbart (1998) explain that attention is a filter that reinforces what is important and undermines distractions. But in the contemporary world, there are a thousand warnings, messages, and online requests that are fighting over this internal attention. Professionals are busier than ever and hardly productive. Thus, the initial stage of intelligent work is learning to control the direction of attention and not its speed.

Figure 5.1: Attentional Focus as a Spotlight

The above illustration shows attention as a targeted ray of light that highlights the significant details and hides the noise. It is the capability of the brain to selectively pay attention to a few stimuli and so it shows how conscious attention improves the clarity, productivity and cognitive efficiency in complex situations where information saturation is a constant capitalist in the attentional process.

The ability of the brain to make choices is what makes human focus. The prefrontal cortex is the manager that determines what thoughts are worthy of being conscious. Perez (2014) asserts that attention is not an act but a skill that is developed with repetition and rest. Once this system is overloaded with interruptions, it becomes inaccurate. Professionals are then left to work hard and get little. The mind is scattered and it switches messages, ideas and screens that steal bits of energy.

A good illustration is that of a software engineer in Bangalore who develops complicated algorithms to logistics firms. At the beginning of his career, he would leave email and chat notifications on all day long because he thought that responsiveness was an indicator of competence. But he realized that he was rewriting parts of code several times due to lost logic. He followed up on his interruptions and introduced a digital silence rule, two hours of undistracted attention in the morning with no notifications. In a few weeks, he was twice as productive, and his error rate was significantly reduced. As his experience demonstrates, attention, after being guarded, is more transforming of efficiency than new tool.

Real attention is relaxed and not strained. Attention is not dependent on paying more attention, it is about removing noise. This can be explained by the metaphor of the spotlight. The beam is only able to shine on a single object at a time. Pashler (2016) argues that the brain is unable to do two controlled tasks at the same time; it switches between them very quickly, and each time it does, it wastes time and energy. Each shift leaves attention residue, residues of the task of the preceding shift that make clarity less clear (Leroy, 2009).

It can take a few minutes to get distracted even when reading one notification. Those professionals who believe that they are effective in multitasking usually go home feeling tired and dissatisfied.

Figure 5.2: Tunnel Vision

The above photo represents the tunnel vision in deep focus. When attention becomes more intense, irrelevant information is forgotten and the person is able to maintain the flow of the mind. The diagram underlines the importance of selective attention that reduces cognitive interferences and improves the accuracy of performance by preventing stimuli that are out of the visual and mental field of the goal.

The experience of flow is also related to focus. Flow is a state of mind in which the balance between skill and challenge is achieved, and action becomes effortless as described by Csikszentmihalyi (1990). In such a state, the focus of attention is constant, and work is meaningful. Without sustained attention, there can be no flow. The delight of complete absorption is felt by a pianist who has lost his place in playing, by a doctor who is examining, or by a designer who is drawing. But interruptions always interrupt before they can start. Individuals who defend periods of deep focus are more creative and less stressed.

Attention science also demonstrates that attention is energy consuming. The brain consumes almost a fifth of the overall resources of the body (Raichle & Gusnard, 2002). This energy is wasted in frequent switching of tasks that could be utilized in solving problems. Professionals should take turns between periods of concentration and conscious rest to save this scarce fuel. Taking breaks, getting deeper breaths, or having short walks replenish the neural activity and do not allow burnout to occur. Such concentration and renewal rhythm is the basis of sustainable productivity.

Focus is also enhanced by purpose. Covey (2020) noted that purpose clarity changes the focus from reactive to proactive. When people are aware of their priorities, or their big rocks, then the mind will automatically focus its light on them. Attention is scattered on trivial things without a purpose; when it has a purpose, it is concentrated on significant objectives. When professionals organize their day according to the main intentions, they minimize confusion and complete work with a feeling of accomplishment.

Environment will either enhance or dilute this spotlight. Visual distraction, noises, or repetitive digital notifications divide attention. The easiest steps to focus on are to close the tabs that are not being used, organize the desk, or turn off notifications, and concentration will get better instantly. Mark et al. (2008) state that even a 20 percent decrease in interruptions results in performance and satisfaction improvements that can be measured. Silence is no luxury: it is order of the intellect.

Practice can also be used to train focus. Creating time blocks, short rituals to begin a work day and creating cues like a notebook or timer, help the brain to know when to capture the attention. These signs form psychological fences which protect the mind space. With time, habit is converted to effort through repetition. What starts as a conscious state of control turns into an unconscious state of preparedness.

Focus is also good in creativity. As opposed to the notion that structure kills imagination, it has been proven that disciplined attention improves imagination. When the brain is focused intensely, associative networks connect far-flung ideas in a better way, creating revelations that diffused thinking can hardly attain. Deep focus does not curtail the creativity- it perfects it. When professionals pay full attention to a single idea, they usually find links that multitaskers fail to notice.

Lastly, attention must be regarded as a cycle, rather than a straight line. Distraction is inherent and the ability to get back to focus is the actual skill. Concentration is enhanced every time the mind wanders and returns. When professionals are patient in their approach to focus instead of punitive, they maintain it longer. It is like musicians who go back to a tune after a break, they maintain balance between hard work and relaxation.

In general, the quality of work and life depends on the spotlight of attention. In this frenzy of the world, and in an unsettled, angry, annoyed one, the art of turning that beam, to an aim, is what there is in the difference between true and false productivity. Professionals create excellence by knowing the limits of attention, insuring it by habit and setting, and focusing it on significant objectives. We do not need silence of the world to focus, we need clarity inside. When the mind is taught to light uniformly on the most important things, all the actions will be deliberate, all the hours meaningful, all the outcomes more gratifying.

5.2 Simplifying Your Mental Field: Reducing Distractions and Mental Clutter

The contemporary mind is confronted with a special problem; it is over-stimulated and under-focused. Alerts, spam messages, the need to be immediate and respond in real time splinter attention. A little vibration or alert appears minute, though combined, it consumes colossal amounts of mental energy. Mark et al. (2008) state that professionals are currently alternating between digital activities in approximately every 47 seconds, which decreases accuracy and creativity. The outcome is cognitive exhaustion-working hard without making any advance. Mental field simplification is the deliberate act of eliminating the inputs that vie against each other in the mind in order to restore clarity to the brain.

There is simplicity, which starts with the ability to minimize thoughts or what is known as cognitive clutter- the varieties of decisions and distractions that take over the mind. Watson (2011) claimed that excessive decisions cause decision fatigue, which undermines judgment and self-control. Each minor decision like opening up messages, switching tabs, or rearranging files is a drain on the limited mental resources. Laborers that develop routines such as set morning schedules or set daily priorities save energy to do high-valued work. Simplification does not depend on doing fewer things; it is about eliminating friction between purpose and action. A plain and simple routine does not create disorder first.

A good illustration is given by a university student in Toronto who was having a hard time with digital overload as she prepared to take her final exams. She noticed that her concentration was becoming shorter as she kept on alternating between social media, class notes, and group chats. She removed all non-academic apps, switched off phone notifications, and started studying in 25-minute Pomodoro sessions to get back on track. In a week, she became less anxious, understood better, and her grades improved. According to her experience, it has been shown that by making the digital world simpler, one can concentrate better than by using any new study method.

Figure 5.3: Concentrated vs. Distracted Brain

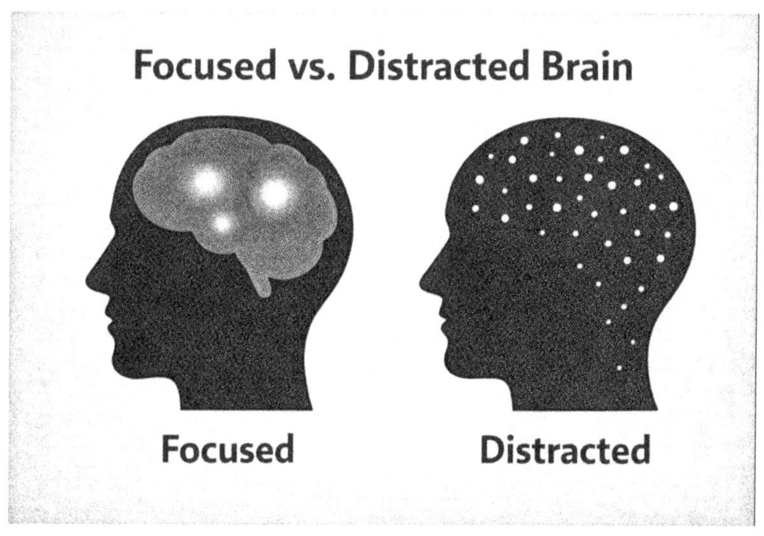

Figure 5.3 juxtaposes two brain conditions: one of a deep concentration and the other one divided by distraction. Neural imaging points to decreased cognitive efficiency in case of multitasking. It shows that focused attention triggers coherent process of reasoning, and divided attention consumes more energy and reduces tasks accuracy and creativity.

There is an enormous distance between a focused and a divided brain. When the mind sets its attention towards one task, neural pathways interrelate with each other in a seamless way which promotes accuracy and creativity. Such paths are not in order in the case of distraction to provide a mental stillness. Multitasking is involved in superficial systems of the brain that are linked to habit, as opposed to deep thinking. This means that the brain is trained to react and not to think. An inattentive person can be called doing a lot but can hardly produce any substantial outcome. Covey (2020) posits that to begin being productive, people ought to start time scheduling the important over the urgent. Clear-cutting must be aware- to do what matters really, and not what makes a strident demand, before it is too late.

Mental clarity is also influenced by physical environments. Noise, messy surfaces, and open browser windows enhance cognitive load and leave the brain with the task of dealing with irrelevant stimuli. In Koundal et al.'s (2022) study, the organized spaces were positively related to quicker task completion and emotional calm. Professionals may also improve concentration by establishing attention zones, special areas or time periods of high concentration work. Mental load separation and dissipation energy release involves relatively easy things like turning off the surrounding noise or cleaning up the desk, and so on. Order is a sign of clean environments and concentration is enhanced by order.

Digital design contributes significantly to making the mental field easier. Each open application and each notification is a rival voice. Cluttered screen is a trigger of micro-decisions, which impairs attention. The counter measure that professionals can apply is to curate their digital tools managing to have one browser open, limiting active applications, and disabling nonessential alerts. Jena and Basu (2018) state that digital minimalism does not mean denying technology but learning to use it. Intentional application of the digital tools makes them friends rather than invaders.

This simplification process is provided with structure by time-based focus strategies. The Pomodoro Technique is a method of work organization created by Cirillo (2018), which consists of 25-minute work blocks separated by short breaks. This is a cycle of balance between intensity and recovery. The mental checkpoint of each completed pomodoro reinforces the capacity to resume the work very quickly after taking a break. Those professionals who employ this technique usually discover that short bursts and focused work are better than long and unfocused hours.

Figure 5.4: The Pomodoro Technique

The diagram above illustrates the time blocking format of the Pomodoro technique, which breaks down work into 25-minute sessions of complete focus with short breaks in between. It demonstrates how concentration and recovery lead to mindfulness, avoid fatigue and make discipline time management sustainable routine of concentration and achievement.

Pomodoro is more effective with the use of digital discipline. Putting notifications on silence, setting device-free time, or using web blockers can ensure that the focus is not distracted by irrelevant information. Aeon et al. (2021) found that planned concentration periods enhance motivation and lessen emotional exhaustion. Frequent breaks do not only help in regaining focus but also provide a feeling of achievement at the end of every cycle. The brain is operating in harmony with its natural ability in this rhythm of concentration and relaxation.

Emotional clarity is also a part of simplification. Most professionals have half-complete ideas in their minds, such as emails to respond to, calls to make, or tasks to finish, which occupy the mind. Recording them or setting them to be released later strains the mind. As explained by Allen (2015), the mind is not a storage system but a creative structure. Any consistent external system - planner, app or journal - releases memory and re-instills peace of mind.

Lessening mental clutter is not only beneficial to the individual but also affects the relationship of the people. Excessive stimulation usually results in impatience and disjointed communication. Professionals who make their cognitive environment simple are better listeners and empathic responders. They are more active in the discussion and teamwork since they are not divided by attention. In this sense, focused attention is a kind of respect.

Emotional well-being is also promoted by simplicity. The mind is inclined to calm concentration when distractions are removed. According to a study by Sonnentag (2018), the organized and calm work patterns promote recovery and life satisfaction. The simplicity that is adopted by professionals allows them to regain mental calmness, the calmness of confidence that is inseparable with the clarity. In a world that means speed is success, simplicity reinvents progress in terms of depth and not velocity.

In general, making the mental field simple is the art of making space to what is really important. Clearing the clutter of all types (physical, digital, and emotional) will help professionals re-get their focus and energy. Well-organized strategies like Pomodoro method, in combination with conscious digital practice, transform disorganized attention into intentional practice. It does not depend on doing more but doing less, with meaning that leads to true productivity. According to Covey (2020), the first step to being effective is to cease reacting to urgency and start prioritizing importance. Here, simple is not nothingness, but transparency, and transparency is the key to sustainable concentration.

5.3 Guarding Cognitive Energy: The Neuroscience of Single-Tasking

The brain is a remarkable organ yet it is not strong enough and there is a limit to its strength. It comprises just two percent of the human body, but it uses almost twenty percent of the total energy

(Raichle & Gusnard, 2002). Some of its functions that are energy-demanding include attention, decision making, and emotional control. Any unneeded choice consumes this valuable asset, and there is less fuel to be creative and empathetic. Neuroscientists thus define focus as a finite battery- it has to be replenished and utilized prudently and not overstretched. Cognitive energy can be guarded, but not necessarily by doing less; it is just more a matter of being more strategic in the allocation of energy.

The multitasking myth continues to exist due to the feeling of productivity that divided attention creates. Professionals usually think that they can handle multiple tasks simultaneously, responding to messages during meetings or listening to podcasts and reading reports. As a matter of fact, the prefrontal cortex is not able to carry out two controlled processes at the same time. Heavy multi-taskers are less effective in filtering distractions compared to single-taskers. Repeated alternate demands put the brain in a state of constant adjustment in changing its focus resulting in what psychologists refer to as the costs of cognitive switching. The outcome is reduced efficiency, increased rate of errors and mental fatigue.

It is a lesson that a hospital nurse in Riyadh acquired through experience. In her initial shifts, she attempted to multitask and manage various duties at once, such as checking patient vital signs, updating electronic records, and answering the phone. At the end of every shift, she was overwhelmed and tended to overlook small details that she had to correct in the future. Her single-tasking has commenced since she participated in one of the workshops on cognitive energy management, where she checks patient records first and then proceeds with calls and schedules to update charts when there are no patients around. After few weeks, she became more accurate, her fatigue reduced and her confidence increased. Her experience is indicative of the fact that single-tasking does not only enhance performance but also brings sanity in stressful situations.

Figure 5.5: Smartphone Brain Drain

Figure 5.5 above illustrates the psychological price of online intimacy. Smartphones even in idle state make the working memory to decrease through distortion of attention. The case can be understood to symbolize the subconscious waste of mental energy

on the online temptation and that is why the boundaries need to be created that would ensure the cognitive energy and maintainability of attention in the workplace.

The environment is also important in safeguarding cognitive energy. Attention can be divided even by silent digital devices. Ward et al. (2017) found that the very presence of a smartphone, even when switched off, diminishes the working memory and focus capacity, otherwise called brain drain. The mind unconsciously devotes mental resources to not checking it, which is a waste of cognitive resources. One way that professionals can protect their attention is to establish clear boundaries: keeping devices out of sight when engaging in deep work, carving out phone-free time, or having certain periods when they should look at messages. Physical distance to distractions usually enhances data straight into mental focus.

The other attention protection strategy is energy mapping, which is the identification and working with the natural rhythm of alertness. Alertness has a biological pattern that depends on light, food, and rest. The majority of adults are most mentally alert in the middle of the morning and in the late afternoon. Without additional effort, it is most economical to align the hard work with these biological highs. As an example, professionals can plan analytical work during high-energy periods and routine or social work during low-energy periods. Thoughtful day takes into account the cycles of the brain instead of struggling with them.

Protecting cognitive energy also involves the inclusion of rest as an aspect of work. The brain is unable to work at full capacity forever. Breaks between activities are short and help to avoid mental exhaustion and renew attention. Small breaks, walks in nature, or moments of silence can help reduce stress and enhance long-term performance. Even a five-minute stroll following a highly stressful meeting or deep work session may reboot neural circuits, erasing neural debris of earlier activities. These breaks are not interruptions, but they are investments in long-term concentration.

Figure 5.6: Deep vs. Shallow Work

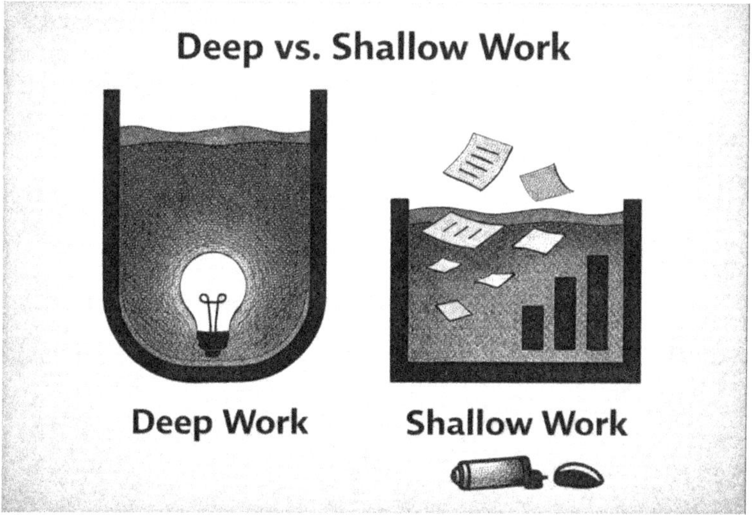

A comparison, such as the one in figure 5.6 above, points out the distinction between the profound and superficial undertaking. Deep work involves concentration of attention on a high value activity whereas shallow work disperses energy on low value activities. The figure illustrates that depth rather than busyness helps to create mastery and creativity as well as quantifiable productivity in both the personal and professional performance.

Deep work entails cognitively challenging tasks of high value, demand full focus, and bear significant outcomes. On the other hand, shallow work involves administrative or reactive work that offers a feeling of motion but not much development. The problem of contemporary professionals is that they have to deal with shallow work most of the day. There is no time to be creative or strategic because of endless meetings, emails, and minor tasks. Deep work enables professionals to maximize the use of their mental peak and create enduring value instead of short-lived gratification.

Neuroscience favors the advantages of long-term attention. Tang et al. (2015) have discovered that regular attention enhances neural connectivity in areas involved in controlling the executive and emotional processes. With time, those who engage in deep focus have better memory, less stressful decision making and are calmer. Conversely, the emotional center of the brain, which is the amygdala, is over-stimulated with frequent switching, resulting in anxiety and lack of emotional equilibrium. Therefore, it is not just about performance, but mental health.

Cognitive energy can be preserved by professionals with the help of systematic practices and feasible planning. Decision fatigue can be minimized by writing down daily goals, grouping similar tasks, and completing one task before beginning another. Even merely closing browser windows or keeping brief intervals of transition rituals between meetings, like stretching or taking water, is a signal to the brain that a task has been completed and there is a new task beginning. Such micro-habits do not allow overlap in cognition, but instead facilitate freshness of mind throughout the day.

Defining success is another way of guarding focus. In societies where speed is valued, rest would pass as laziness. However, studies indicate that the most successful people in various professions, including athletes and executives, operate in brief, sharp bursts and then take breaks. They know that it is not the number of hours, but quality attention. Safeguarding attention is thus neither a weakness nor foolishness.

In general, smart working is all about cognitive money. All distractions, choices, and machinery consume some of it. Individuals who learn to single-task, to schedule their activities in accordance with the natural rhythms, and to safeguard attention by taking rest, accomplish more in less time and with less effort. The point of guarding focus is not perfection, but precision, applying the brain intelligently and operating within its boundaries instead of pushing them. Sustainable excellence is a part of the world that is addicted to speed, but not intensity.

5.4 One Thing at a Time: The Myth of Multitasking

The contemporary culture tends to idolize the multitasker, the individual who can write reports and respond to messages at the same time, attend to meetings and respond to emails at the same time, and manage deadlines without so much as a beat. Multitasking is regarded as an indicator of efficiency and dedication in most workplaces. However, studies have shown time and again that what is perceived as productivity is in fact a distraction. Rubinstein et al. (2001) state that task switching may increase completion time by twofold and the error rates by threefold when performed frequently. The working memory of the human brain is only capable of one controlled process at a time. When individuals split their attention, they do not work faster, they just alternate faster between tasks, losing focus with each alternate.

The perception of multitasking is due to the fact that the brain confuses movement with progress. Every new activity results in a feeling of stimulation that produces a little rush of dopamine the same neurotransmitter associated with pleasure and novelty. This is not only satisfying in the short run, but it disrupts focus and competence over time. The continuous alternation of tasks overloads the prefrontal cortex and creates an attention residue, a residual thought of the last activity that disrupts the next one. Multitasking eventually reconfigures the brain to engage in superficial work, and deep focus becomes more difficult to maintain.

Multitasking in the workplace can manifest itself in the form of divided presence. A manager who reads emails in a team discussion may seem efficient but he or she may not get the tone and context. When a teacher grades assignments and responds to student messages, he or she splits not only time but also empathy. Biased attention compromises both the quality of work and relationships. Perez (2014) states that the most important type of focus is presence, which involves complete attention to the current moment.

Single-tasking is what gives back substance and focus to thinking and connection. It enables the brain to handle one stream of information to the maximum before proceeding to another. The lesser the cognitive activity in the working memory the more coherent the neural activity and the faster the learning and more accurate performance of the activity. The accomplishment of a task itself is an intrinsic reward on its own: the dopamine release reinforcing the drive towards the next objective. On the other hand, the incomplete assignment is stressing and tiring as a person does not have time to finish the multiple tasks, and the workers feel busy and under-satisfied.

Figure 5.7: Chase One Rabbit

Figure 5.7 above was inspired by this proverb: If you pursue two rabbits, you will not find either of them. The idea is that divided attention is meaningless. It is an image of wisdom in following one thing at a time and single-tasking helps to be clear about the goal, effective and calm-headed than befuddled by multitasking.

The intelligence of the one rabbit principle, which is based on an ancient Chinese saying, is in deliberateness. It teaches that when one tries to achieve several things at the same time, he or she will become mediocre, but when one concentrates on a single priority, he or she will excel. There is a tendency of professionals to conflate between activity and achievement and to think of movement as progress. Nonetheless, as Covey (2020) noted, focus needs courage, the courage to say no. You must choose what you want to be your top priorities and be bold enough, and it is pleasant, smiling, and unapologetically, to say no to other things. Intentional attention is not constraint but freedom--it puts the power into that which is really important.

This change was witnessed by a marketing executive in Singapore. She has been working on ten projects at the same time over the years because she thought that multitasking was a sign of leadership. She had meetings, messages, and mental switching all day long. Even though she worked long hours, her deadlines were missed, and she was less creative. She was frustrated and decided to cut down on the number of campaigns she was going to do to three rather than ten. In a month, her performance was significantly better-every project was given more attention and her team was giving better results. Focusing on simple things, she not only became more productive but also managed to gain confidence and peace again. Her story shows that the most fruitful choice that one can make is to say no to excess.

Such stories are supported by the science of single-tasking. Tang et al. (2015) demonstrated that long-term attention enhances neural networks that are related to decision-making and emotional regulation. On the other hand, multitasking over-stimulates the brain stress center (amygdala) which makes one to feel irritable and fatigued. Single-task professionals have fewer mistakes, shorter durations of work, and are more stable psychologically. The advantages are not limited to the work place; concentrated people claim to have better memory, more meaningful discussions, and feel more balanced.

Technology tends to promote the exaggeration of a temptation, multi-tasking. The illusion of control and stealing attention within several micro seconds are a result of smartphones, open tabs, and notifications. Each ping or vibration entices the brain into the reactive state and it is required to make a decision whether to respond or not. This constant vigilance in the long term wears out the brain. Professional can solve it by defining the area of focus-disabling irrelevant notification, setting do not disturb, or single-purpose devices at work such as during important and serious moments. They reaffirm their control on digital demands by creating conducive environment which is supportive to depth.

Another advantage of single-tasking is that it enhances the leadership and relationships. During a meeting, whole hearted leaders develop trust and create psychological safety. They are in unceasing existence, an indication of a noble and hospitable approach to sincerity. Conversely, split attention conveys the message of indifference albeit without any failures. The professionals do not get interrupted in hearing and hence perceive not only the words but also the tone, emotion and nuance. Attention has then been viewed as a form of empathy, complete attention on others.

The move toward single-tasking has major implications at an organizational level. Research reveals that multitasking in the workplace lowers productivity within teams, which leads to a communication bottleneck and redundant work. Those firms that implement organized focus times, during which the employees have continuous work, record more innovation and satisfaction. Deep work does not decrease collaboration, but instead, it improves it by enabling people to bring quality insights instead of fragmented input.

Overall, neuroscience cannot pass the myth of multitasking, nor can experience. When the human brain is engaged in one activity, it is working in its best capacity. Professionals who do single tasks are more efficient, they do not make many errors and they are more pleased with their work. It is not in multitasking that one is really efficient but in single tasking. It is true to the saying: When you chase two rabbits you will not catch any of them. In a world that values speed, the last thing that one would desire is to take his/her time and do everything with precision and attention.

5.5 Building a Focus Routine and Mindset

Attention is not part of one personality, but a habit developed and achieved by repetition, surrounding and contemplation. The focus is also comparable to a physical stamina and improves with practice and rest. The modern profession involves un-countable distractions, yet individuals who use conscious focus training become excellent at the points at which the rest of the populace is distracted. It is not done by strict control that should be built but by developing a pattern that preserves mental energy and allows flow.

Starting with a powerful emphasis routine is the morning structure. A clear high-priority task at the beginning of the day creates momentum that affects the rest of the day. Morning is a psychological anchor; the morning will make or break the day, with purpose or lack of purpose. Individuals who wake up purposefully (with journaling, goal review, or morning affirmations) in the morning, condition their brains to be leaders rather than reactive. This is not to do a lot but to begin meaningfully.

One teacher from Nairobi created such a routine because of the problem of fatigue and divided attention in remote teaching. The way her mornings would be is to check messages, review lesson plans, and prepare materials at the same time. The continuous changing exhausted her even before her classes started. Her concentration and tolerance toward detail became more pronounced after enforcing an organized schedule the quiet breakfast, 10 minutes of deep breathing, and listing the three primary teaching objectives. Her students said that her lessons were more understandable and relaxed. She has had experience that when attention is paid early in the day, the whole day is geared towards clarity and not chaos.

The morning rituals though, do not constitute the entirety of focus-building. The role of mindfulness is also crucial. Creswell (2017) states that even brief daily mindfulness practices improve long-term attention and emotional control. Mindfulness enables professionals to be aware of distraction before responding to it. Even a simple two minutes breathing technique that is performed between meetings during commutes can re-set the brain and melt in the tension that has been built up. According to Perez (2014), mindfulness changes the autopilot to awareness, which enables people to act in a thoughtful manner, as opposed to acting impulsively. This consciousness is the basis of deliberate attention.

The focus cycle is completed by reflection. Routines can easily become habitual without any review and instead become mechanical. Reflections can take place on a weekly basis to allow one to look at the period of where the focus went and the cause which led to it and how this can be reestablished. Aeon et al. (2021) have found that practitioners capturing their concentration patterns, including time of the day, the type of distraction, and emotional state, describe positive performance and satisfaction that is measurable. Meditation transforms mistakes into something to be used, and suffering into light. To keep refining routines, a brief end-of-week journaling session, which poses the following questions will help. What worked well? What caused me to lose attention?

The other side of focus is recovery. Without conscious rest, attention is impossible to maintain. Mental recovery, particularly physical activity, exposure to nature, or creative hobbies, restores energy, creativity, and emotional stability. When it comes to recovery, professionals tend to confuse it with laziness, which is not the case. Giving oneself a brisk stroll after a working day, listening to music or spending time with family members reestablishes the attention systems of the brain. Rest is a sustainable productivity and not an exhausting one when it is incorporated into a focus routine.

It is also possible to do focus routines intentionally with the use of technology. They can be used as accountability tools rather than fighting vehicles by professionals. To improve on time spent on focus and to avoid multitasking, one can apply Forest, Focus To-Do, or Rescue Time. According to Jena and Basu (2018), the trick is that one should plan distraction instead of avoiding it altogether. The reduction of the sense of guilt and recovery of attention can be achieved by professionals by assigning certain time restrictions to emails or social media. The head gets a relief when it feels that the distractions have their place.

The above attitude is also supported by environment design. Ordered surroundings carry emotional ease and cognitive efficiency. Professionals may establish focus areas, such as special desks, quiet areas, or noisy-free libraries. Cognitive load is minimized even by minor environmental stimuli like good lighting or comfortable seating. The brain identifies these spaces with concentration, and the focus becomes activated faster with time.

This mental association is strengthened by rituals. The transition to deep work is marked by a pre-focus ritual this could be clearing the desk, setting up a candle or put on headphones. Csikszentmihalyi (1990) explained that rituals assist people to get into the state of complete immersion known as flow, when effort is natural, and time is lost. These cues condition the mind to transition to engagement with distraction easily.

Boundary communication is also a part of establishing a focus routine in professional life. The deep work hours should be known to colleagues and clients. Establishing a definite availability time can ensure they are not interrupted all the time and that respect is developed among each other. Focus norms are beneficial to all in workplaces where open communication is encouraged. When an individual explains purposeful attention to others, it usually motivates others to follow in their ways.

Focus mindset is associated with acceptance, emotionally. Distractions are unavoidable; the point of focus is not to avoid them but to get back to it as soon as possible. Tang et al. (2015) state that long-term concentration strength is determined by the capacity to resume attention following disruption. A concentrated individual is not a person who never loses his track but one who returns to his track with grace again and again. Such an attitude eliminates the feeling of guilt about lapses and makes attention management a humane practice.

Lastly, the attitude of gratitude strengthens the focus attitude. Taking a few minutes at the end of every day and writing something that one has accomplished or something that has given meaning to his or her day in some way fosters intrinsic motivation. It reminds the professionals that growth is maintained by progress, not perfection. This emotional closure helps avoid burnouts and enhances optimism, which is the fuel to the mind to focus on the future.

In general, the creation of a focus routine is a self-leadership activity. Influencing attention through design of mornings, mindfulness, weekly reflections, and protection of recovery professionals, make recovery more of a regular beat than a battlefield. The story of the Nairobi teacher demonstrates that order brings calmness. Focus routines do not inhibit creativity; it is freed by removing noise in the mind. As Aeon et al. (2021) proposed, when people focus on purpose, they not only become productive but also peaceful. Real concentration does not have anything to do with the control- it has to do with the alignment of power, consciousness, and vitality.

5.6 Chapter Summary

Attention is the basis of any significant success. Living in the ever noise-saturated, notification-filled, and mentally cluttered world, people who learn how to focus their minds gain power to manage their time, energy, and inner tranquility. Attention is a spot light - when directed willfully, it is a good way of bringing things into focus and blurring those out of focus. Focusing ability is not a mere cognitive ability but a choice.

This chapter discussed the importance of clarity of attention in making the mundane seem extraordinary. Reducing the mental field simplifies it and eliminates distractions in the mind. The preservation of cognitive energy is one of the ways to make sure that the small resources the brain has access to, are spent on productive tasks instead of being spent on switching programs all the time. Single-tasking enables people to get back into thought and enables professionals to accomplish tasks accurately, creatively, and satisfactorily.

Every character throughout the chapter (the Spotlight of Attention to Chase One Rabbit) represented a lesson in learning how to focus on things deliberately. They demonstrated that attention does not concern itself with reducing the possibilities of life but rather putting forth the possibilities through intention. The development of habits, mindfulness, and rest make the attention to a stable cycle instead of an acute spurt.

Finally, intentional attention results in flow, which is skill and challenge in harmonious effortlessness. Work is transformed into art, time is slowed, and meaning enriched in this flow. Learning to be focused does not turn any person busier, it only improves him, and it is the living testament that the clarity, rather than the chaos, is the ultimate measure of productivity.

Key Takeaways

- Any meaningful work is based on focus.

- Distractions can be minimized which saves mental energy.
- Single-tasking promotes insight and focus.
- Minimal practices guard against cyber overload of attention.
- Reflection brings back balance and clarity of mind.

Weekly Tasks

1. Set all sources of needless notification to silence during the day.
2. Create one mental session (free of multitasking).
3. Clean up your workspace then begin your next work.
4. Become aware of when you are the most focused and match important work with that.
5. Withdraw as an end, look back at the day, and see what caught and lost your attention.

Chapter 6: Hack 5—Optimize Your Environment

Half unconsciously a chaotic atmosphere steals attention before it takes any action. Even the environment surrounding you influences the way your mind will work, although this is not obvious. Human beings tend to pursue discipline, productivity software and inspirational speeches but forget the chair, the light and the background noises dictating all ideas.

Mackey (2024) states that ergonomic comfort has a direct effect on cognitive endurance and mood: ergonomic discomfort and low-light conditions are associated with fatigue, pain, and distraction. The reality is so plain and clear, your environment is your silent accomplice to success or your untold hindrance.

Nowadays, work occurs anywhere: desks at home, cafes, offices, airports. According to Robertson et al. (2013), efficiency improves when the environment is in accordance with the natural needs of the body. Being in a supportive environment lets go of the willpower needed to focus energy on creativity. To optimize space implies adjusting what is visible, what is felt, the height of a desk, the air quality, temperature and even the sound texture. All the factors contribute to or deter mental clarity.

Environmental design is not the decoration, but the engineering of behavior. It is possible to create reminders to your brain by purposefully creating your environment in a particular way that reminds you of what you need to remember to do. Just like the preparation by the athletes before they play, people perform well when the workspace, which is the office, is harmonized.

The sections below discuss the ways to create that stage first by developing an efficient physical environment, then arranging the objects and digital resources, and the last idea is to watch how one individual managed to turn messiness into order. Together, all these strategies demonstrate the idea that you change your surroundings and your output changes.

6.1 Creating a Productive Workspace

The first step to start a productive working environment is with comfort and clarity. The environment in which an individual works determines the effectiveness of the mind. The brain is also maintained by the environment, which supports the body. When individuals are sitting in awkward positions or trying to view their screens, some of their focus is always redirected to pain or balance management. In the long run, pain consumes attention and reduces motivation.

Supian et al. (2023) state that even minor ergonomic changes like changing the height of the chair or the location of the screen can greatly decrease musculoskeletal pain and enable workers to be more attentive to longer durations. Thus, as properly designed working area conserves cognitive effort. The body is able to relax instead of fighting fatigue and the mind is able to think without any problem.

Ergonomic set up brings about balance between posture and performance. The monitor must be at eye level to ensure that the neck is not tilted. The elbows must be at an approximate right angle, the wrists straight and shoulders loose. When straining is to be avoided, feet should be placed flat on the floor or resting on a footrest. The natural curve of the back needs adequate lumbar support to minimize fatigue in the long sitting hours. Lighting, too, matters deeply.

Natural light is preferable since it enhances alertness and mood, however, where this is not possible, soft diffused lighting can be used to ensure the eyes remain comfortable without glare. According to Mackey (2024), the optimal work temperatures are 20 to 25 degrees Celsius. Excessive heat makes one slow, whereas cold air makes muscles stiff and less dextrous. All it takes is a little heater, fan or an open window to get the comfort back without being costly. As the physical environment feels at ease, the concentration will be easier and prolonged.

Another crucial concept is that of having a place that involves work-only. Divergent mental boundaries are maintained by separating professional activity and rest. Even a plain table in a quiet room will make the brain realize that it is time to concentrate. Robertson et al. (2013) argue that behavior is influenced by environmental cues in terms of association.

The brain develops patterns; over time, a specific seat, smell or lighting condition triggers productive work. This association is confused by working on the same couch as watching movies or scrolling through social media. This is then opposed by the mind as the space is a symbol of relaxation rather than hard work. Even a cheap desk is a visual representation of intent. When you sit there, you get into a psychological workspace where concentration automatically increases.

It is not just the sight and posture that determine productivity, but the other senses also play a role in performance. Sound may either sustain or discontinue thought. Silence is perfect to some people, whereas soft instrumental music or background noise can be used to cover unexpected distractions by others. Constant background noises (rain or cafe conversation) provide an acoustic veil that assists in keeping attention.

Scent is another element that can form mental state, although it is mostly ignored. The slight scent of citrus can be used to wake up, whereas lavender can be used to relax and concentrate. Associative memory is developed by using the same scent during working hours. Then, after a while, the simple act of smelling it is enough to set the brain in concentration mode, as an exercise war-up. These sensory components convert space into an experience: a collection of indicators, which make your mind take the task at hand in its entirety.

An empty room may be chilly and uninspiring. Human beings work best in environments that portray their identity. Personal objects remind you of the reason why you are working and what you appreciate. Zhenjing et al. (2022) state that employees who customize their workspace are more engaged and satisfied as they feel a sense of ownership and have control. Yet balance is crucial. Excessive decorations cause clutter and less focus whereas well-selected ones are comforting and motivating. A photo of your loved ones in a frame, a green plant or inspirational quote can be a silent reminder that you have a purpose.

Plants are especially beneficial, as they not only improve the quality of air but also alleviate stress. Even a splash of color such as a bright pen holder or a patterned notebook can be used to lift mood in long hours albeit subtly. Individualization must create enthusiasm, rather than dissipation. Each thing must be worth its name by either being utilitarian or making us feel stable.

Lighting does not only define visibility, but also mood. Low lighting is a burden to the eyes and leads to headaches. Position the light sources in such a way that they are on the side and not directly behind or in front of the screens. When you can, put your desk by a window, since being exposed to natural light helps to maintain the circadian rhythm of the body, which increases daytime activity and nighttime sleep. As the light of the sun diminishes, the warm artificial light maintains a warm feel of the room without lighting bright shadows. Other individuals have adjustable lamps to regulate the brightness according to the time of the day. A small room can be turned into a welcoming and stimulating place with proper lighting.

Beauty is also observed in a productive workspace. An attractive space improves the mood and promotes longer and more pleasant working hours. However, never should beauty be at the expense of function. Calm is produced by clean lines, a clean surface, and careful choice of color.

It has been found that blue colors promote concentration and stability, whereas a little bit of green stimulates creativity. Do not use over stimulating colors like bright red around your desk as this may cause tension. The best designs are a combination of soothing colors with some elements of warmth, maybe wood textures or soft fabrics, which make the room look human and not mechanical.

Figure 6.1: Aligned to Productivity

Figure 6.1 above represents the effect of physical placement on the mental performance. A comfortable workspace that is well lit and in a good posture will facilitate long term concentration. It indicates that when the body is supported, and the surrounding has removed distraction, productivity increases, and the effort turns into a kind of rhythm, and a focus becomes a natural and continuous state of mind.

When the physical space coincides with the psychological intent, work is not 'hard work' but a rhythm. You are no longer struggling with discomfort or distraction, the room itself promotes the state of mind needed to succeed. A good working environment is not based on luxury but on balance, comfort that keeps you going, order that keeps you thinking, and a personal touch that helps you remember why you are doing what you are doing. With a deliberate effort to mold the environment to your body and mind, you will have a place where concentration is natural and productivity is not forced.

6.2 The Role of Organization and Minimalism

Organization takes disorder and turns it into order. Each misplacement, pile of paper or cable quietly drains psychological resources. When the brain is faced with clutter, it needs to process each object seen in it, including the ones that are not pertinent to the task. Trajkovic et al. (2025) posit that the brain attentional networks are overwhelmed by visual clutter, which makes them re-focus their attention.

On the other hand, minimalism generates mental space. It eliminates unneeded decisions and visual clutter that makes the brain focus on what is really important. The properly arranged space is not only comfortable, but also a working device of concentration, imagination, and relaxation.

The obvious basis of productivity is physical order. Begin cleaning the workspace of your desk and leaving only such necessary objects as a computer, a notebook, and maybe a water bottle or a pen holder. The drawers, boxes or shelves should be clearly labeled in order to easily retrieve all the other materials. By having the tools in their respective place, there is no need to think to find them and the brain is able to think of something new instead of wasting time seeking supplies.

This order is reinforced by a brief end of day reset. Take five minutes to clean up paperwork, put back pens and to get rid of garbage. Prepare necessities of tomorrow before departure. This minor ritual is an indication of a close, and the psychological division of work and rest. Since the routine is something you get used to, it does not allow you to accumulate it, and you start each day with fresh energy. Even hours of cleaning save up to hours in a year.

The psychological advantages of simplicity are scientifically proven. Kruk et al. (2018) established that orderly spaces promote selflessness, healthier behaviors, and more resilience. The rule is simple enough; external order promotes internal order. A disorderly room is a scattering-room; an orderly one a collecting-room. However, minimalism has nothing to do with de-cluttering life. It is concerned with conscious ownership--keeping only that which fulfills your cause, and getting rid of what does not.

Minimalism is not a pleasant style, rather it is tactical in a professional environment. Crippling redundant equipment, redundant files, or ornamentation never kills personality, but only signifies will. Everything that remains to be seen is justified. The simplicity which is abandoned presents a feeling of control and self-confidence and it makes the visitors and the owners feel competent and composed.

Physical and mental stress are decreased by hygienic environments. One of the things that cause a bit of anxiety to the brain is a messy room since it leaves the brain reminded of things not done. In the situation where the environment appears out of control, there is an increase in cortisol levels, which is the major stress hormone of the body. This is worsened in home offices where the personal and the professional conflict. The things are cleaned up and a mastery is restored. In cases where there is no surface or reality with which to relate to, then that will be closure and not disorder that is seen by the mind.

Organization will also aid in reducing decision fatigue that is energy robber. There cannot be small decisions when everything is where it belongs. You do not waste time any longer in seeking a paper or where to locate your pen. All the decisions that are saved make the complex thinking be listened to. The growth of these micro-efficiencies over time reaches a high growth of daily performance.

Figure 6.2: Clear Space, Clear Mind

Figure 6.2 above explains how minimalism enhances clarity of mind. Cleaning space does not only remove distraction but also makes decisions that are not worth making and also focuses on the work that is required. Clean space helps to alleviate stress and promote relaxation of mind. The aesthetic simplicity has increased the control and discipline and the outer order has been changed into the inner intent and the psychological calmness.

Minimalism is more of identity than efficiency. The less is more, is a statement of simplicity: you know what is the most important. Minimalism is the retention behind that which arouses joy, but in the case of professionals the incitement to progress. All the swept out drawers are definitions of themselves. The process question is: which are the tools, books or habits that are actually serving my purpose? Why do I retain anything, because I do it as it is custom or because I feel guilty of it?

This is where the aspect of minimalism is not a denial against this light but the power source. You do not like divided attention and will and you do not like extravagance, you like economy. The emptying of a room containing the room aids conveys some silent message of sternness. It is a masterpiece that is silent, and it implies that it portrays a feeling of expertise to all access points. Physical simplicity is a digital information overload revolution, and it is possible to know that less is more.

Order should be enforced not presupposed. Organization is not a cleaning spree but it is a system which is continuous. One would do it in the simplest possible categories that are able to characterize your working process: a file, or a folder of incoming items, another of active work and the third is of completed archives. This assumption is true in the online world. The time that would have been wasted in the search process would be saved by installing the documents in transparent folders according to the project or date.

Consistency is the creation of reliability. The orderliness in a situation, where the direction of things is determined by the routines, is not a thing to work towards. As a muscle, Minimalism is accretional in that it builds up through drilling. The more you have been accustomed to putting things back, the better it is. Several minutes of daily attention will prevent extreme messiness that makes it necessary to hire cleaning crew during weekends. The order is not a thing, but a way of life- a way of life that will reward hard work with rest of mind.

Organization plays a crucial role in influencing emotion. A tidy desk and an open-table are signs of relaxation and potential, respectively. When there is reduction in visual noise, creative thinking is increased. An open environment makes abstract thinking easier as it frees the working memory of irrelevant stimulus and this is what the researchers observe in the study of cognitive psychology. Neither is the structure nor the silence hostile to creativity: the conditions are conducive to creativity.

Even the burnout can be insured by a meager working room. Unrest is not a customary practice of this tumultuous era. The sparse environments are considered as a visual rest station and in such environments, the mind is able to re-set after an undertaking. They also bring about pride: when you take care of your space means that you take care of your work. The cleaning then becomes more of self-respect than a kind of coercion because of this psychological form of slavery.

Figure 6.3: Empower Your Space

Figure 6.3 above is a symbol of the unity that has been achieved between totality and minimalism. It portrays that everything in a working environment is helping to build stability, confidence and the feeling of emotional security. A harmonious atmosphere fosters creativity and serene concentration when there is a balanced atmosphere and hence the working place becomes a place where clarity is perceived rather than where there is confusion and discipline is applied automatically.

The mixture of the two features is minimalism and order to form psychological safety the unspoken rule of being in a steady and manageable condition. This stability is conducive to concentration. This is because the perception of everything that possesses time and space and order is predictable and creates confidence. With this sense ground it liberates the mind to devote its utmost attention to complex problems.

To sum up, minimalism is a philosophical position. It implies that you not only take care of what is around you but also take care of what you are thinking too. Anything that is preserved proves to be a deliberate move to add to the concentration, harmony, and the development. When the discipline is one with the clarity of the inner world displayed in the world of appearance, there will be no imposing discipline on it- there will be a natural agreement. Through minimalism, your workspace is no longer a room; a mirror of the systematic that you learn to create in yourself.

6.3 Digital Environment Optimization

A neat desk is pretty small when the screen before it is disorderly. In the modern world, the work environment is much more than physical furniture; its dimensions become computers, phones, and clouds. The contemporary employee works a greater part of the day with the involvement of digital devices, and they influence the efficiency of the mind functioning.

The state of screens that are full of tabs, notifications, and unread messages increases mental clutter despite having a clean appearance. Ohly and Bastin (2023) claim that productivity may reduce by half due to continuous digital distractions. Each notification requires a response and the brain has to switch gears and redefine focus every time again and again. Alerts are meant to command attention unlike the background noise which can be tuned out. The more they occur, the less the concentration is sustained.

Structure is the easiest way to go digital. A computer should have folders and naming systems just like a clean room requires drawers and shelves. Sort files based on project, client or date depending on your personal style of working. Keep what has been finished, get rid of what is no longer needed and do not allow the miscellaneous folders to turn into digital junk drawers. Unsubscribing to useless mailing lists and getting rid of unused applications relieves the mind.

The rule of touch-it-once used in paper documents is ideal in email management. Whatever you receive through a message, you can make a choice as to whether to reply, file, or delete. This would avoid the accumulation of undelivered messages which silently take their toll. Having a clear inbox lowers stress levels since it is an indicator that there is no urgent matter concealed. This habit saves time in the long run as well, which could otherwise be used to re-read old threads. The overall outcome is a smooth communication and increased control.

The interface clutter is the virtual counterpart of a cluttered desk. There are far too many icons, browser tabs, or open apps to see. Streamline by organizing similar applications into folders and deleting the short cuts that you hardly utilize. A few professionals use bare-bones launchers or focus modes, which conceal all the tools except the tools used. Other people would assign different desktops to different activities, such as writing or other communication or research, so that visual representations of the workspace correspond to their mental concentration.

The act of closing idle tabs saves memory space in the computer and more importantly, human energy. Every open tab is sort of an unfinished thought, pulling a bit on focus. Tabs of the background take up memory and divide attention. Making the screen simple enables the brain to recognize what is of most importance; thus multitasking can be divided into sequential single-tasking. This is a rhythm that has been proven to be more accurate and efficient.

Active delimits are necessary to control attention in the digital age. Turn off social media, news, or any other unrelated chatting sites, auto-synching, and social media pop ups during work hours. Frontzkowski et al. (2025) argue that multitasking slows down the accuracy and time taken to complete a task since the brain is unable to process complex tasks fully in parallel mode. Each distraction leaves a cognitive residue that cannot be forgotten even after one shifts focus to the primary job.

Rather than being responsive at all times, schedule the communication windows twice a day. During those times, use them to read and reply in a reflective manner as opposed to being impulsive. Silence the noise the rest of the time. This batching methodology is receptive of other methods employed by professionals who perform well to recapture deep concentration. In the long run, it reprograms the brain so that it is resistant to reactive checking. You are the one who decides when to be connected as opposed to being called on each ping.

Continuous contact may be viewed as control, yet it mostly becomes enslavement. Individuals bring their work with them everywhere in life checking emails during dinner, updates before sleep. Kushlev and Dunn (2015) discovered that the frequency of emails sent to a person can be significantly reduced to lessen stress levels and boost satisfaction. The human brain needs rest in order to congeal memory as well as to build emotional equilibrium. Continuous partial attention, but, keeps it at alertness, which is exhausting of its energies that ought to be refreshed at rest.

Digital minimalism is a way of bringing boundaries back. Choose the time when devices work to your benefit but not the other way. Switch off the screen when eating or taking a break and think about phone-free mornings to shape the day in a peaceful manner. The outcome is increased concentration at work and relaxation when out of work. The states can be improved when there is a transition between the intensity and rest of the mind.

Figure 6.4: Tame the Digital Chaos

Figure 6.4 above describes the way digital order improves productivity. It demonstrates that distraction and fatigue can be avoided through managing files, turning off the notification, and

using digital tools in a simple manner. An ordered screen resembles an ordered desk, and technology should not be a distraction but enhance profound focus to improve a seamless integration of digital systems and human consciousness.

The other optimization level is the skill of using the tools. A large number of professionals use software in their day to day tasks without even considering its efficiency. Friction can be minimized by learning keyboard shortcuts, automating repetitive actions, and developing templates of the most used documents. As an illustration, an email signature template would save seconds that would translate into hours per year. Spreadsheet macros and project management automations and quick-access folders make operations even more streamlined.

The time spent learning your main tools will be multiplied many times over. The executive part of the brain is optimized when it is repetitive in nature and becomes automated. When you have tools that run well, you are able to focus on creativity or analysis. The working environment at that moment transforms into a collection of devices into a smooth system that assists in mastery.

There can be no digital order without digital safety. Copy files on cloud storage or external disks on a regular basis. Loss of work due to failure of hardware or accidental loss is not merely an inconvenicnce, but also, it causes emotional strain and time wastage. The use of strong passwords and multi-factor authentication secures data as well as peace of mind. Security gives confidence and you can go about whatever you want without the fear that something will disappear.

Software should be updated periodically in order to resolve vulnerabilities and performance. Eliminate old programs that drag systems. Take care of your devices as you would your work mates- keep them in good condition in order to deliver their best.

The best environments make the two worlds compatible. A real world desk planner reflection of your online calendar is one way of bridging the gap between physical and computer organization. The process of handwriting important objectives strengthens the memory and associates the abstract plan with the physical location. Equally, naming digital folders in connection with the paper folders avoids any confusion in one medium to another. Analog consistency with the digital order makes the whole workflow a single unitary system and not two opposing worlds.

In the end, there is a clear digital space, which reflects a clear mind. It does not depend on learning to use technology but rather about becoming unseen, technology is put into the background, and thought becomes the focus. Once the realm of the digital order and the physical organization are aligned, productivity ceases to be a fight over the control and it becomes a natural manifestation of peaceful efficiency.

6.4 True-to-Life Scenario: Workspace Makeover

Being a software engineer of thirty-four years with the home in Madrid, Miguel found himself in a loop of exhaustion and distraction. After his company had transitioned to working remotely, his apartment served as his office, but it was not made to be productive. The television and the refrigerator were placed between his desk and the wall, and the light cast a lot of shadows on the screen and his phone was vibrating on and on next to the keyboard. He spent many hours working online, but his code reviews were getting more and more, and his creativity was getting lower and lower. He later said that he thought he was not motivated but in reality, his environment was not helping him.

The first thing that Miguel did was to bring his desk close to a natural light window and to eliminate the rigid dining chair in favor of a seat with an adjustable ergonomic design. He placed the monitor at eye level and placed the keyboard in a way that the wrists were flat. This change was instant- no neck ache, the reduction of headache, and greatly extended deep concentration. The modification followed Supian et al.'s (2023) study that found ergonomic comfort to be associated with mental endurance.

Figure 6.5: Adapting Structure when Needed

Figure 6.5 above shows how movements to ergonomics change concentration and vitality. It shows that even minor modifications in the chair height, the amount of lighting and the position of the screen can alleviate stress, decrease the fatigue and enhance creativity. The design is based on the principle that flexible and well-designed environments can help develop endurance in the mind and long term professionalism.

Then Miguel addressed physical clutter. His desk was now a dumping ground of receipts, chargers and take out boxes. He took a whole afternoon to clear his surfaces and to put only the necessary things there to code his laptop, a notebook, and a cup of coffee. He included a small tray of wood on which cables and devices could be placed. The air was less dense and so was his concentration. As Trajkovic et al. (2025) found, visual clutters also take the neural processing power; their absence allows the brain to do more serious work.

Miguel then made some selective personal additions. He had a framed snapshot of one of his hiking trips in the Pyrenees on the wall; a reminder of balance and perseverance. The presence of a small cactus by the monitor brought life without any need of care. He did not go overboard with decoration, following Zhenjing et al.'s (2022) prove that lower personalization raises well-being without causing excessive attention. The effect was a cordiality of not to be distracted; a sterility of not being orderless.

The most significant obstacle was the digital anarchy. On Miguel's desktop, the numbers of files and folders named new, final or latest were hundreds and his email was full of messages that had not been read. He started by establishing a well-organized folder structure: Projects, Clients and Archive. Another strategy that he introduced is the inbox-zero, whereby he answered or archived messages on the spot. To reduce distractions, he turned off social media notifications and silenced Slack notifications unless there was an urgent thread in the team.

The effect surprised him. It was strange to be silent at first, but then he saw that he was able to think again. He also discovered that a higher reduction in the frequency of being notified leads to lower levels of stress and performance enhancement. The productivity of Miguel doubled in weeks not due to an increase in his working hours but due to continuous working.

Figure 6.6: Draw the Line

Figure 6.6 above interprets physical and mental boundaries between work and rest. It emphasizes the need to stop work rituals, such as closing laptops or switching lights to indicate relaxation. These changes ensure emotional stability, refresh motivation, and safeguard mental health to ensure healthy and consistent productivity.

The last thing that Miguel did was to draw the line between work and rest. He used to code at night and even check messages in bed. He had now made a ritual, at half-past six he shut his laptop, put it in a drawer and turned up the room light to a cozier color. Switching off his computer became symbolic, a visible sign that a workday is over. His chair was even placed on the opposite side of a table at dinner so that he could not get attracted to his job by visuals.

This border enhanced his mood and sleep. Research proves that work and personal separation zone increases well-being and avoids emotional fatigue. The deliberate separation of his space of body and mind allowed Miguel to reclaim his evenings, and gain creative energy the next day.

After securing the fundamentals, Miguel took the environment as a living system and no longer a fixed set up. Monthly, he made a review of what was working and what required change. He found out that a mixture of sitting and standing sessions enhanced circulation and that a small afternoon walk helped to make him more alert in the late afternoon.

He also tested background sound a few times- jazz and other times silence, and followed the conditions which corresponded to his concentration rhythms. These continuous improvements also manifested what Adiga (2023) referred to as micro-ergonomic evolution in which minor and continuous enhancements keep performance at a high level.

In two months, the condition of Miguel changed so that he was in a position of 'disorder to order'. His activities were completed at a quicker rate, his body position was better, and his performance of stress was reduced. He referred to his workplace not as an office but a thinking studio. The difference was evident to visitors, the room exuded not fatigue but cool efficiency. His transformation proved one of the key truths about productivity which states that quality of output is quality of environment.

The case of Miguel gives an idea of one of the principles that most human beings overlook, which is, success does not begin with motivation, but design. By returning to his surrounding he moved into the reactive action to the intended action. Every light, object and silence served its purpose. Productivity to him was no longer a question of the amount he could accomplish but of how his component parts were synchronized, both physically, electronically and mentally, to the activity of which he most highly valued himself.

6.5 Chapter Summary

Optimizing environment implies the creation of behavior within space. The first step is starting with the physical. Optimizing an environment is converting space into a resource that facilitates productive behavior. This first step is the physical comfort, the posture, lighting, and temperature that make the body up to date and the energy consistent.

It reaches into organization and minimalism, in which neat environments clear the eyes and the mind. Digital order is a follow-up of that transparency, its result being fewer notifications, properly arranged folders, and any screens without distraction. All these layers make a system of the ecosystem in which concentration is not imposed but rather natural.

Any change: an ergonomic chair, a marked-out drawer, or a dulled phone, gets rid of tension between desire and action. According to Adiga (2023), individuals shift their environment to suit their needs, which contributes to higher performance and, consequently, the well-being. The area that develops consistency is pleasant and serene and the one that needs much correction is disorganized.

The concept of this hack is delicate but powerful: turn productivity into the design of the surrounding environment and do not simply employ discipline. Learn to have the chair remind you to sit well, the desk in the picture to create focus and the blank screen to make the flow moving. A well designed environment does not compel you to excellence, but makes excellence the path of least resistance. It is in that simplicity that there is productive permanence: permanent, effortless, and reconciled with attention and calmness.

Key Takeaways

- Environment silently shapes behavior and focus.
- Physical comfort enhances energy and performance.
- Minimalist design reduces mental clutter.
- Digital order sustains calm and efficiency.
- Thoughtful surroundings make discipline effortless.

This Week's Task

1. Declutter one surface in your workspace today.
2. Adjust your lighting and posture for better comfort.
3. Disable one source of digital distraction (like pop-ups or notifications).
4. Add onc environmental cue that reminds you to focus (a timer, a quote, or a plant).
5. Reflect on how your environment affected your attention each evening.

Chapter 7: Hack 6—Cultivate Self-Discipline

This is a well-known paradox of every professional: "we are aware of what really matters, but we do not always do it." The gap between intention and execution is what self-discipline has to fill. Hoffman (2017) explains that self-discipline is a skill and not an inherited attribute, but a product of repetition, reflection, and responsibility. It is the unseen power that turns aspirations and dreams into objectives and outcomes. Discipline is not subject to mood and circumstance like motivation, but to fatigue, boredom, and distraction.

Figure 7.1: Ulysses Pact

The picture in figure 7.1 above depicts the old concept of a commitment device, acting intentionally to avoid temptation in the future. Similar to Ulysses tying himself to the mast to overcome the Siren, contemporary professionals employ pre-commitment tactics like deadlines, contracts, or online restrictions to protect attention and still have self-control in a stressful situation.

Developing discipline in the contemporary world requires order and self-knowledge. It is does not just depend on motivation but the direction, the decision to move forward and not to stay in the comfort zone every day. McGonigal (2013) argues that discipline maintains performance by saving willpower by designing the environment strategically and thoughtfully. The disciplined individual does not just depend on motivation but creates mechanisms that ensure that doing the right thing is easier than doing nothing.

Emotional intelligence is also in practice discipline. It is the control of impulses, concentration and quick recovery after lapses. An Accra teacher planning lessons, a Dubai coder debugging a program or a Manila medical intern working long hours all have to face the same reality: inspiration rarely leads to success.

7.1 Overcoming Procrastination with Practical Techniques

One of the most everlasting foes of progress is procrastination. It masquerades itself as harmless procrastination, but it is full of emotional avoidance. Kuhnel et al. (2023) explain that procrastination is not so much a time management issue; it is an emotion management issue. When something is too daunting, too uncertain, or too uncomfortable, the mind finds a way of escaping it in the short term by looking away. Reviewing messages, cluttering the desk, or excessive planning is a psychological way out. Every procrastination makes a loop of guilt, stress and doubt; however, and it is multiplying.

The process of self-discipline starts when people get to learn how to free themselves of this emotional pattern. To beat procrastination, it does not need force but clever mechanisms or methods that make doing something more comfortable than not doing it. Implementation intention is one of the effective strategies, a method that converts the naked intentions into definite promises. An example is, one does not say, "I will work on my project soon, but, if it is 8:00 a.m., then I begin with the project outline." According to Duckworth and Seligman (2017), such if-then statements are methodical because a behavior connected to the intention is directly associated with its context. They decrease mental negotiation making a decision a reflex.

Another technique that is equally effective is micro-tasking, which involves the breaking up of big, threatening objectives into small but immediate achievable steps. This approach is the one that puts the mountain aside and focuses on the first stone. The psychological momentum comes with one paragraph typed, one folder cleaned or one email sent. Every minor success releases the chemical of rewards, dopamine, which motivates one to do more. Micro-tasking professionals turn the anxiety into advancement, since they do not wait to become ready anymore but begin small and get clarity as they do.

Figure 7.2: Cue the Habit

Figure 7.2 above explains the way cues evoke automatic behavior, depicting the process of cue, routine and reward which are involved in the formation of habits. It represents the visualization of the way of stimulated action by certain triggers, such as time or place or visual cues, and the way rewarding completion enhances repetition. The model illustrates the process in which discipline becomes an automatic process with purposeful cue design.

The other foundation of getting out of procrastination is environmental design. Oymirzayeva and Murtozayeva (2024) pointed out that behavior usually comes after the environment rather than intention. One has to make desirable actions easier and undesirable distractions harder in order to enhance productivity. An example is of a Nairobi lecturer who always delayed grading, but she had an easy fix with an intervention; she would leave her checklist and marking pen in full view on her desk before leaving her classroom. As she went back the signal was unspoken. Her rate of delay in grading reduced by 40 percent in one month. Her surrounding turned out to be a friend rather than a challenge.

The same principle applies to the digital spaces. Cognitive clutter can be avoided by arranging the work tools to facilitate easy access and reducing notifications. According to some research on behavioral psychology, every digital distraction involves the cost of a few minutes of orientation. Focus apps, browser blockers, or quiet phone modes are examples of things that can be used by professionals to minimize temptation. As Inzlicht et al. (2018) described, willpower is finite; therefore, it should be saved. The smart design minimizes the self-control that one requires all the time since it entails discipline built into the environment.

Time-anchoring is another technique which is practical. Association of a new task with an existing routine aids the brain to associate action to a familiar rhythm. As an illustration, one can make a decision after the morning coffee, such as, "I will check my project timeline", or after lunch, "I will respond to main emails." This practice makes habits sequences and not acts. Studies indicate that behavior based on the day to day occurrences is absorbed quickly due to the ability of the brain to predict it. Time-anchoring proves to be very practical to the busy professionals whose time is unpredictable since it brings discipline to the natural procession of the day.

An even more psychological weapon is the Ulysses Pact, an approach to pre-commitment referred to as such after the Greek hero who bound himself to the mast to avoid seducing by the Sirens. The modern one is where one commits oneself beforehand to not procrastinate in the future. This can be by creating a set time of publishes, downloading applications which block distracting sites, or informing fellow students about the date of project completion. The uncomfortable sense of responsibility is a factor that makes unspecified goals tangible commitments. McGonigal (2013) suggested that pre-commitment helps to make internal conflict less since it prevents tempting one to commit a sin before the temptation occurs. An example is a writer in Johannesburg who announced at one time the week-by-week publishing dates on social media. The slight social pressure became discipline and her consistency doubled.

Although systems and cues play an important role, the process is finalized by emotional regulation. Avoidance is aggravated by many procrastinators who engage in self-criticism following failure to meet deadlines. Self-compassion; realizing there is no shame in struggle, is a better motivator in less time than guilt. The productive people perceive lapses as feedback and not failure. Minor failure is an experience, but not a vice.

The simple three-step model of reflection that may be applied by professionals after a lapse consists of: (1) Identifying the emotional trigger (fear, fatigue, perfectionism); (2) Accepting it kindly (It is okay to feel uncertain); (3) Take one small step. Such attitude avoids paralysis of the emotions. In the long term, self-compassion will establish resilience, which is the capacity to come back to discipline following disruption.

Neuroscience of action is an advocate of such practices. Charness et al. (2024) state that every time individuals overcome their reluctance to act, the prefrontal cortex of the brain enhances its muscle over impulsive circuits. That is, all follow-through rewires the brain to be consistent in the future. The brain learns that pain is a transient condition whereas pleasure is permanent.

Finally, the most disciplined people are not those who do not procrastinate at all, but those who get up fast when they fail to do so. They establish habits that guard attention, settings that lessen enticement, and mindsets that translate loss into advancement. These layers build a system of responsibility and elegance over a period of time.

Overall, procrastination does not clear itself out upon pressure, but by a design. The willpower is substituted with systems, the guilt is substituted with cues and a sense of disgust with the self is substituted with self-compassion. Action becomes natural when it is emotionally safe, contextually guided and socially confirmed. The discipline of self-starts where procrastination ceases just at the same point when the individual decides to do something regardless of the uncertainties and this proves that it is the courage that forms the foundation of progress rather than perfection.

7.2 Building Sustainable Discipline

The art of always keeping track no matter how moody, tired, or distracted you are is called discipline. Charness et al. (2024) claim that sustained focus does not happen due to punishment or strict control but due to alignment through which motivation fits well with the identity and purpose. Real discipline is maintained because people establish a system that minimizes tension between the will and the action. It does not involve pushing behavior as much, but rather creating a setting, mode and habit that intrinsically encourage following through.

The root of long-term discipline is the formation of identity. Oymirzayeva and Murtozayeva (2024) noted that individuals respond better by transforming their thinking pattern in a way that they are no longer outcome oriented ('I want to exercise') but identity oriented (I am a person who values movement and health). Action has a meaning in identity. Resistance is reduced when behavior is congruent with self-concept. This was implemented by a medical student in Cape Town when he was preparing to take board exams. She did not rephrase, but rather refocused her mind from, "I have to study" to "I am a future clinician learning to save lives." This minor change turned the compulsory into the prideful and the regular into the identity. Every study session was the confirmation of who she was transforming to be, not a task to get done.

Figure 7.3: Identity-Based Habits

This character depicts the way self-concept determines continuity of behavior. The identity circle that is the inner one leads to the repetitive habits that in turn strengthen the identity. It illustrates that perceiving self-image as one contributes to the consistency of actions that one performs in their everyday life and makes daily activities the mirror of who a person is and not what should be done.

Energy management is also a determinant of sustainability. Grant and Shandell (2022) discovered that willpower is more like a muscle, in that it becomes exhausted during overuse but rejuvenated during recovery. The professionals who are conscious of this rhythm maintain long term discipline by planning rest, nutrition and social interaction. According to Albulescu et al. (2022), the employees who had planned micro-breaks reported higher persistence and emotional stability throughout their working week by 23 percent.

They were not putting in more time, they were putting in a better way by switching on and off between work and rest.

One of the nurses in Doha incorporated this lesson into her timetable by spending ten minutes between rounds of patients to stretch, hydrate, and reflect. The regularity assisted her to maintain concentration throughout the long shifts and avoided burnout. Sustainable discipline is therefore not the unremitting stand but the moderated enjoyment.

Figure 7.4: Temptation Bundling

Figure 7.4 above illustrates the effect of combining a pleasant action with a challenging one on the results of following through on it. Through mixing up pleasure with discipline, like music when working out or coffee when doing paperwork, the mind learns to tie effort with reward and this is where a good feedback loop will be formed, which will keep the person motivated in the long run.

Temptation bundling also uses the reward principle of psychology. One client, a project manager in Kuala Lumpur, was so fed up with repetitive financial reports that she only listened to her favorite podcast during the completion of those reports. Gradually, her brain characterized the task as something relaxing and exciting. What was formerly dull was satisfying. She achieved naturally and without being forced to complete her reports. This strategy shows that consistency is achieved when working is not a punishment but a reward.

Sustainable discipline is also learning to delay gratification, which is the capacity to focus on the long-term results rather than comforting the present. A study conducted by Moffitt et al. (2011) revealed that people with high self-control experience a better life and success many decades after that. But in the world where humanity is obsessed with speed and has to be constantly stimulated, patience is radical. The modern employee is bombarded with the flow of instant gratifications, in ways of emails, likes, and updates that shorten the time to focus. The power of waiting is, therefore, one of the capabilities reclaimed by sustainable discipline.

This principle is incorporated in the actions of a teacher in Accra who would get materials of the lessons ready, two weeks before. She gets relaxed, innovative and in control where the others are busy getting things done by the end of the day before classes. She understands that there should be nothing like tomorrow carried out without planning the present. The discipline will allow her some freedom and this fact goes to show that not indulging in gratification is not deprivation but self-respect.

Figure 7.5: Power of Grit

Figure 7.5 is an embodiment of the idea of perseverance as the driving force of discipline. It symbolizes the way in which long-term consistency can turn short-term suffering into mastery proving that grit, which is the combination of passion and persistence, can help an individual to endure hardships and attain significant objectives by repeatedly being value-oriented.

Grit is what binds all these together. According to Hoffman (2017), grit can be characterized as the ability to persevere and be passionate about meaningful things. Moral professionals can stand the test of time since they do not rely on discipline that is mechanical in nature. It is not imposed, but adopted. A Nairobi social entrepreneur had explained that the reason she was working long nights in keeping the community projects logistically active were not sacrifices but acts of service. The strength that she had was her ability to persist even when she was tired because she saw a vision in the form of enhancing access to education.

Sustainable triad of discipline is therefore a combination of energy management, purpose and identity. When action is informed by a sense of sharpness of self and purpose, both the efforts reinvigorate motivation and do not exhaust it.

Flexibility is also required to sustainability. It has been suggested by Mesman et al. (2021) that adaptive goals are those that change as the situation changes and these maintain the motivation more effectively than set targets that are inflexible. The professionals that adjust their strategies according to changes experienced do not burn out. Sustainable discipline is not stagnant; it is always changing its approaches without altering the mission.

Consistency may also be supported by technology in a wise manner. Reminders, time-tracking tools, and digital calendars ease the cognitive stress so that professionals can concentrate on implementation. However, tools should serve form and not substitute meaning. The disciplined person applies technology as scaffolding, rather than a replacement of purpose.

In general, sustainable discipline is a combination of identity and energy with purpose in a harmonious system. It is not the ruthless conflict of the will power but the beautiful beat of habits that agree with the meaning. When we are acting in the way we want to be, then we feel that persistence is natural. A disciplined man does not struggle in the same battle day-to-day- he just lives in relation to his chosen identity. Sustainable discipline does not depend working extra hard, but creating life in such a way that effortlessness is made.

7.3 True-to-Life Scenario: From Chaos to Discipline

At a busy design company in Seoul, two of the colleagues: Min-Seo and Liam had the same workload yet they experienced very different work rhythms in their lives. They were talented, creative, and ambitious, but they had the same day approaches, which influenced their success in opposite manners. In a hurry, Min-Seo was in the habit of checking emails, giving clients news, and opening project boards in the morning, and that was only after that, she was able to design work. Her day went by in instalments, the distraction keeping her more and more out of time. Fatigue replaced satisfaction at night. During the day she labored and produced little of value. On the other hand, Liam had begun every morning deliberately silent. He prepared coffee, spent twenty minutes creating whatever he desired and glanced at his task board and opened his inbox. His mornings were silent and his attention exceedingly tardy. Their performance varied and this became evident in a few months.

The transformation that has taken place in Liam did not happen by chance. He had decided many months ago that there was a scheme of accountability partnership since he was fed up with the inconsistency. On each Friday, he and a co-worker, Hana, would go through their weekly objectives in ten minutes. The sessions were in an informal yet regular manner. They discussed improvements and assessed time wastage, and planned on the following week.

The results were venture-level. The same was supported by Harkin et al. (2016) who found out that the rate by which the goal is achieved increases by 42 percent through monitoring of the public progress. A goal becomes psychological when it is expressed. Accountability transforms the individual will to that of social contract, enhancing the structure and the group responsibility. Liam did not have to depend on personal will only; he had structures and overall responsibility to rely on to make him consistent.

People were encouraged by his consistency as weeks went by. Min-Seo, who had been constantly busy with many things to the point of exhaustion, became interested as to why Liam remained so stable. She noticed that his production was not through frenzied effort, and she inquired of him how he did it. He told her about his routine and the rule to begin small but remain constant. When she got her morale boosted, she enlisted the help of a coach to coach her on her procrastination habits and she learned about the two-minute rule, whereby since the task takes less than two minutes, then it is good to do it without delay. This productivity expert rule has been confirmed by behavioral researchers to reduce decision exhaustion by avoiding indecisiveness.

The change was observable in a few weeks. Min-Seo did not allow emails and sketches to accumulate but immediately handled small tasks, providing mental space to be creative. It was not a dramatic but gradual improvement, and every completed micro-task gave confidence and minimized stress. Evenings spent by her ended with successful closing rather than disorder.

The workplace was not spared in the change. Liam was motivated by their achievements and introduced a new office culture, which he referred to "Focus Hours." These two daily periods were when team members muted notifications, took a break and focused on one key task. At first, there was a silent resistance to the idea. Others were afraid of less cooperation; others did not believe that it would last. However, in a month, performance figures were better. The projects progressed quickly, revision rounds reduced, and employee satisfaction surveys showed 20 percent increase in reported focus quality. Focus Hours became part of company policy by the management.

Discipline was no longer an individual practice but it was a culture. The design team found that structure did not kill creativity as it helped to develop it. The decision to engage in a creative breakthrough usually happens once the sustained concentration is overlaid with the intentional rest. To be able to create complex ideas, the brain needs continuous immersion; the constant changing in between is a killer of depth. The team was able to access greater creativity in fewer hours by securing some creative time.

The change was reflected in Min-Seo's development. At the end of her workdays, she would and still does make a list of three achievements and one thing she wants to improve and then closes her laptop feeling like she has made a step forward. At the end of the year, she was promoted as an assistant designer to a project head, leading two high profile campaigns. In his turn, Liam was promoted to the position of creative director, which included mentoring of junior designers.

Their collaboration went on. They continued to review goals (not out of necessity, but out of habit) every Friday. What had begun as discipline had become complementary stewardship or progress. They failed to meet their meetings occasionally but never lost momentum as failure to keep accountability had become a cultural- not a conditional- issue.

Figure 7.6: Accountability Partners

Figure 7.6 above describes how disciplining systems based on mutual commitment, peer relationships, or mentors, can be able to work together. It demonstrates how regular check-ins will produce integrity, motivation, and monitoring of progress that will alter individual accountability into an interdependentness that will produce steadiness overtime in either professional or personal desires.

The narrative of Min-Seo and Liam draws three universal facts about discipline. First, there is discipline by contagion. When done in a free and open manner, it maintains itself by observation and imitation. Witnesses of composed consistency unconsciously attempt to do it. Second, accountability changes effort to reliability. As the purpose is communicated, and monitored, people change their mindset of intent to performance. Having at least one accountability partner increases the chances of follow-through. Third, structure safeguards creativity. Discipline does not curtail innovation and, on the contrary, it provides the permanence required of the imagination.

It is reflected in organizations all over the world. The same concept is exploited by remote teams relying on digital tools of accountability, such as shared dashboards, or academic cohorts that make weekly peer reviews, all of which implement the same principle of progress: where visibility and responsibility are combined, progress is bound to occur.

The last thought that Min-Seo had when she attended a team seminar, summed up what the two of them had undergone through: “I have always believed that discipline was about control,” “Today I perceive it as care, care of my time, energy, and trust of my team.” Her lines summarized the fact in Hack 6: discipline is not hereditary. It manifests itself in rituals, routines and relations that are more concerned with consistency rather than intensity.

The Seoul Company was then known by the following quarter due to its innovative design flow and culture of teamwork. Their success case went viral to affiliate offices in Singapore and Tokyo, where the Focus Hours and accountability concept was shortly copied. The change was referred to by the leadership of the firm as a silent revolution of rhythm and respect.

Overall, discipline is a matter of choice and a social phenomenon. Once accountability, emphasis on respect, and demonstrating composure become a norm among teams, the individual habits of team members become consistent with the overall excellence. The disciplined environment becomes self-maintaining, a culture where productivity becomes natural, creativity is enriched and mutual trust is exercised instead of micromanagement. Discipline will not be imposed in such an environment; it will become the common beat of significant activity.

7.4 Long-Term Strategies for Resilience and Grit

Discipline cannot be established by habit; it is sustained by emotional perseverance. However, with time, the most effective systems are faced with fatigue, doubts and failure. It is not in skill that those who survive and those who give up differ but in stamina. According to Hoffman (2017), grit is the key to perseverance and interest in long-term goals. Whereas talent is a catalyst of performance, grit is a daily sustenance of performance due to hardship. In real resilience, professionals can be able to flex under pressure not to snap, not to lose the purpose.

Discipline is a long term factor depending on the capacity to control emotional healing. Most specialists confuse guilt and growth because they think that self-criticism that is mean and hard, makes one more responsible. Nonetheless, according to the research conducted by Perinchery (2023), guilt is not an indicator of quick behavioral recovery in case of mistakes but rather self-compassion. Guilt is energy-consuming and reflection rejuvenating. When one reacts to mistakes with a sense of learning instead of feeling ashamed, he or she maintains an incentive to make the next attempt.

Figure 7.7: Guilt Spiral Vs Self-Compassion Loop

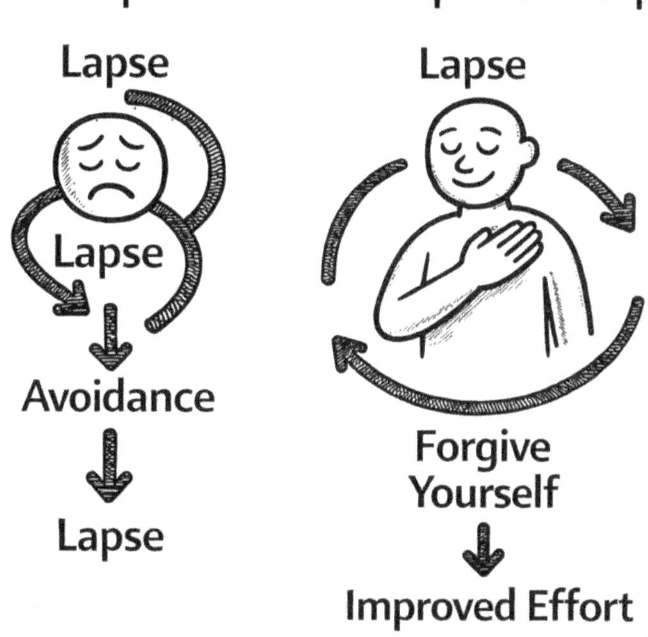

Figure7.7 above compares two mental processes after failure: the downward spiral of guilt that increases avoidance and exhaustion, and the upward loop of self-compassion that supports learning, emotional stability and motivation. It shows the speed at which self-forgiveness helps to build resilience and maintain progress in the long-term.

The common characteristic of professionals who learn fast to overcome their failures is that mistakes are just information, not identity. They consider failure as a process commentary and not a character commentary. One of the civil engineers in Mombasa, having wrongly managed a project schedule, started writing a journal of all the lessons every week rather than dwelling on mistakes. In three months, her project performance improved, and her stress decreased. Failure was converted into success by the power of self-forgiveness coupled with the process of reflection.

Resilience is also developed with the help of adaptive goal-setting. Goals approached as flexible, but not fixed, help individuals stay more motivated as they get disrupted (Mesman et al., 2021). When people face failure, they reposition as opposed to withdrawing. This strategy was represented by a startup founder in Lagos when his company was struggling with economic turbulence. He did not give up on his quarterly goals, instead he re-packaged them in an achievable priority: client retention, cost optimization and team morale. Such a lax position rescued the trust and the aim of his team, and made it possible to recover gradually. His ambition was not deterred by any kind of flexibility but rather made it sustainable.

The long-term attitude is critical in the long-run resilience. The Institute of Education Science (2022) claims that growth-oriented thinkers do not consider difficulty a failure, but view it as feedback. Persistence will be self-reinforcing when it is viewed as an opportunity to develop. Strong personalities are not those who escape pressure, but those who perfect a reaction to it. An example of this is when a university lecturer in Nairobi who was waiting for promotion was trained to view peer review as a form of collaboration and not criticism. The rotation made them less protective and ameliorated the learning. Resilience is a cognitive redefining strength, which is formed in consciousness.

The other techniques that increase grit are reflective journaling, mindfulness meditation, and physical activity. Mindfulness training enhances the augmentation of the anterior cingulate cortex in the brain managing the emotions and attention in the state of stress (Charness et al., 2024). The concern is brought to the journal and rumination is brought into clarity. Endorphins are released in the process of exercising; thus, stabilizing the mood and energy. Together, all these practices act as shields during turbulence; they bring sanity such that one is able to continue.

Social reinforcement of resilience also takes place. Man is never meant to live in seclusion; affiliation will enhance power. Professional networks, mentoring circles, and faith-based groups are known as communities that serve as emotional scaffolding under community. According to research, workers who claim high levels of social support have 35 percent greater persistence in the face of high workload pressure. Cognitive endurance allows emotional safety. By having professional backing, the professionals can take risks, fail, and rise again without the fear of being rejected.

Take the case of a nurse in Manila who participated in a peer reflection circle at the time of the pandemic. She and her colleagues talked about issues and coping mechanisms every week. This started as a survival group and later turned out to be a professional development community. Members would support each other to come up with micro-goals, win, and suffer setbacks. With time, their strength in terms of resilience as a group became more effective than the fatigue of each of them. The group dynamics help discover that perseverance is more than an individual work effort: it is a social structure.

Purpose alignment is also a great idea with long-term discipline. Eshiett and Eshiett (2025) found that intrinsic motivation, or working toward the goal of personal values caused a stable level of dopamine, and less emotional burnout. Professionals who can directly relate their day-to-day work with something important in their lives, which could be creativity, service, or mastery, feel more satisfied and less exhausted. Even the most boring task maintains attention in a teacher who considers grading as essential to produce future thinkers or in a coder who considers their task as creating digital accessibility. Value changes work into reason: it is a source of perseverance in times of loss of motivation.

Under the influence of emotional intelligence, resilience acts as a renewable resource. Instead of trying harder, tough guys and girls know how to get back smarter than before. They work their minds as athletes work their bodies by resting, adapting and conditioning themselves. They learn to be graceful during failure, flexible when uncertain and grateful because of the effort. These are the emotional components of sustainable discipline.

In the evolving organizations, resilience is a communal need to develop. Organizations that lead by encouraging change through open discussion of failure are psychologically safe, and those that train individual effort are the ones that promote long-term commitment. Employees who are perceived positively and appreciated due to their resilience and performance are more retentive and creative. A survey of workplace well-being shows higher resilience programs are promoted by companies that record 30 percent lower turnover and 25 percent higher innovation scores.

Lastly, the longest lasting practice is the self-compassionate grit, which is a type of determination that is based on kindness, as opposed to strictness. It embraces imperfection as part of the progress and does not take the rest as weakness or preparation. Strong professionals know that recovery creates resilience and not fragility.

In general, resilience is not a genetic gift, but a self-management move. By being friendly to oneself, setting adaptive objectives, engaging in mindful recovery, and relying on supportive networks, grit can be replenished. A disciplined man is not the man who never stumbles but the one who learns quickly and rises more prudently and proceeds more benignly. Compassion, rather than control, is what keeps one going in the long run.

7.5 Chapter Summary

Silent power or self-discipline makes success meaningful and lasting. It fashions mere intention into conscious action, changes chaos into order, and pressure into productive rhythm. This chapter showed that procrastination is not a character failure but an emotional reaction to discomfort- the one which can be reformed using cues, context and less judgmental structure. According to Oymirzayeva and Murtozayeva (2024), successful discipline is established in systems that facilitate doing things right and discourage doing things wrong.

Figures 7.1 to 7.7 represent these lessons, the Ulysses Pact leads to pre-commitment to goal, to the Guilt Spiral vs Self-Compassion Loop, which represent the renewal of motivation through forgiveness. Collectively, the images highlight the fact that good discipline is about being tough and at the same time understanding. The practical examples of Nairobi, Kuala Lumpur, and Seoul show that strictness is never natural: it is acquired, exercised, and enforced by the surrounding environment and responsibility.

Sustainability is a result of identity and coincidence. Professionals who consider consistency as a statement of being and not doing also maintain the advancement without straining a lot. The combination of structure and renewal, ambition and rest, and resilience and reflection creates a sustainable rhythm that supports steady growth and balanced achievement.

As Hoffman (2017) found out, our biggest achievements are not related to intensity but to consistency. The disciplined life is not fixed; therefore, it is not inflexible, it is rhythmic and rooted in purpose, but bendable in approach. Developing discipline is not merely a professional necessity but a life time art: the day-to-day decision to develop, continue, and act willingly, although comfort may be beckoning him or her to stop.

Key Takeaways

- Discipline is the daily act of aligning choices with long-term goals.
- Consistency matters more than intensity; small, steady habits shape character.
- Rest and recovery are essential parts of sustainable discipline.
- Self-control increases focus and emotional stability under stress.
- Environments that support order, clarity, and accountability strengthen discipline.

Weekly Challenge

1. **Track one habit** – Choose a small action (like journaling or morning exercise) and do it daily for seven days.
2. **Design your discipline space** – Remove one distraction from your workspace and add one cue that promotes focus.
3. **Set a daily cue** – Link your disciplined behavior to a time or trigger (for example, "After breakfast, I will write for 20 minutes").
4. **Reflect nightly** – Spend five minutes reviewing what helped or hindered your focus during the day.
5. **Reward follow-through** – Celebrate each day you keep your promise to yourself, reinforcing progress with positive feedback.

Chapter 8: Hack 7: Reflect and Improve

"The unexamined life is not worth living." – Socrates (Miller, 2020).

Efficiency does not have a definite destination; rather it is an ongoing cycle of learning, adjusting and developing. Once one has learnt the art of planning, prioritizing, and focusing, the second critical step would be reflection, a habit of transforming experience into knowledge. The gap between improvement and doing lies in reflection. It takes everyday behavior and makes it conscious by posing three guiding questions: What worked? What did not? What would I do differently the next time?

Di Stefano et al. (2014) argue that the reflection on a regular basis improves performance due to the strengthening of self-awareness and enabling people to draw conclusions based on everyday experience. Reflection does not allow busyness to turn into stagnation in personal and professional life. It opens the eyes, builds resilience, and enhances living with purpose. Reflective people always develop at a greater pace, as they do not hesitate to look at their victory as well as their hardship.

Hack 7 is the final element in the circle of efficiency that promotes the mentality of continuous improvement. Every review-be it daily, weekly, or monthly establishes a feedback loop that converts the errors to lessons and habitual practices to permanent routines. Reflection does not require hours or even formalized reports, it only takes curiosity, honesty and a few minutes of conscious consideration. Reflection makes moments of action moments of learning so that nothing happens in vain. It repeats every success, every failure, every day, a little test in growing better, not in growing more active.

8.1 The Power of Regular Self-Assessment

The process of self-examination, which is the act of stopping to examine actions, decisions and their outcomes, is the starting point of reflection. Slowness in thinking is an infrequent virtue in a world where fast action and conspicuous consumption are prized qualities. As indicated by Di Stefano et al. (2014), people who spend fifteen minutes daily and engage in structured reflection enhance their performance more than twenty percent. Reflection is effective because it transforms experience into knowledge and enhances meta-cognition, the awareness of the way one thinks, makes decisions and learns. It does not just enable people to act but also to find out the sense in what they do.

Introspection is the act of placing a mirror on the mind. It transforms the smog of everyday life into a very vivid and visible image that can be used to make more informed decisions. Most of the hard working people spend their days in reaction, but not observation. They work effectively but hardly bother themselves to find out whether tasks they do are important or what they can do to improve them. With reflection they start to see patterns, when energy is high and when distractions happen and when the situation is conducive to inspiration or when it is conducive to fatigue. Consciousness is the starting point of betterment.

An evaluation of oneself does not necessarily need to be multifaceted and time-consuming. A ritual every day of a few minutes can amass tremendous gains. Even ten minutes of sincere examination at the close of each day can help to sharpen the eye better than hours of mechanical drill. One of the most common frameworks used to frame reflection is a three-question model:

1. What went well today?
2. What could have gone better?
3. What will I change tomorrow?

Such easy questions will change the focus of judgment to learning. They emphasize achievement, point out what is wrong, and make instant conversion of knowledge into action. With time, a feedback mechanism of self-evaluation makes the decisions stronger and eliminates the need of unhelpful habits becoming habitual.

Reflection is a curious rather than a critical task. It is research, not analysis. The attitude of a researcher instead of a judge makes reflection easier, when an individual comes to self-assessment. An inquisitive mind would question itself why something worked and not why one failed. This level of inquiry maintains the morale at a high level as it reveals data to be improved. Patterns start to be noticed in the course of several weeks- maybe the productivity is more active on those days when people exercise in the morning or are much more fatigued after the days of multitasking. When the patterns become visible, they can then be redesigned.

Figure 8.1: Daily Reflection Mirror

Figure 8.1 above demonstrates that the effectiveness of short-end-of-day journaling enhances self-awareness. In the image, the individual is writing short notes based on three questions: what went well, what to improve, and what to change. It is a symbolic reflection of the mind that transforms daily experience into learning and makes awareness a regular learning practice.

Reflection is not about an individual alone, but the source of professional culture across the globe. Reflection is built into companies in Japan through the process of hansei 37, a formal meeting that is conducted after each project to review the process and attitude. Nonaka and Takeuchi (2019) explain that hansei demands participants to accept what has not always been successful, with or without triumph. Instead of sharing a sense of accomplishment, they talk about what went wrong, what the reasons are, and what they have learned before beginning a new undertaking. It is not to blame but to progress. Through introducing humility and flexibility into the working process, organizations are able to make sure that they include reflection in their DNA.

The other evident case is in the healthcare. Placed at the end of a patient rounding or a clinical procedure, reflective debriefs take place on a regular basis between nurses and doctors. These meetings get a planned break within a stressful environment because teams may ask a question of what worked, what could be improved, and how safer care delivery can be attained. Epstein and Krasner (2013) argue that professional judgment and empathy are enhanced by this reflective practice, which is accompanied by a reduction of professional burnout. Studying caregivers, the caregivers revisit a sense of purpose as well as streamline their expertise and mercy.

Reflection also helps in resilience. Contemporary life has a tendency to put individuals in a state of urgency where busyness is substituting improvement. Fatigue and repetition can conceal downfall without any conscious examination. Self-assessment disrupts that trend, by making one look back. Every contemplative moment will serve to protect against mindless activity. It brings sanity and makes people think of what is really important.

Reflection should be part of everyday life in order to make it sustainable. A habit coupled with another habit lasts longer. Close the computer by writing three sentences at the end of the working day. Educators may write down one observation in the classroom; entrepreneurs may recap one lesson in business; parents may write down one thankful experience. Once reflection develops to be as routine as brushing your teeth or glancing at in-mail, it turns into an additional activity and then becomes a natural rhythm.

Technology may help but not rule the process. There are those who choose journaling apps or digital planners; and those who choose pen and paper. The approach is not crucial but the attitude. People should not be afraid of writing by hand since it can slow their thought to the extent of inviting depth and sincerity. The only thing that is important is that reflection occurs regularly and with integrity.

In the long run, the periodic self-assessment will yield apparent growth. It can be seen in the previous sections of this book that the thinking process becomes more focused and the envisioned issues become smaller, and self-confidence grows. Reflection creates a silent kind of responsibility the awareness of the later review of decisions stimulates better actions at present. It develops a sense of humility in order to admit mistakes and bravery to rectify them.

In all professions and cultures, the message is the same: reflection makes experience the expertise. Its application might not be practiced in the company of a factory in Tokyo, or in a hospital in Nairobi, or even in a classroom in Toronto, but the principle is universal. Any person who takes time to examine himself or herself becomes more deliberate, flexible, and balanced.

Connecting reflection and everyday life, any person can transform self-assessment into a refreshing or an inspiring process instead of a burden. Even the few minutes of silence turn movement into meaning. Month by month, they create a roadmap of improvement--a visual document of development and strength. Life no longer becomes a whirlwind of events and turns into a conscious road to mastery through the rhythmical movement of reflection.

8.2 Learning from Failures and Adjusting Methods

Any real growth will incur failure. It is inescapable that every individual who strives to become better will experience times when things go wrong or the result is poor. However, those moments of shame are reframed through reflection. According to Edmondson (2011), the most effective organizations consider mistakes as information and not a weakness. When there is psychological safety at workplaces, individuals are able to openly investigate mistakes with no fear of embarrassment and punishment. The same principle is applicable to personal development: it depends on how one reacts to the failure of it to turn into a teacher or a trap.

When failure comes, it is never fatal, but it is often final. In the background of each failure is feedback to the systems, habits or attitudes that must be honed. Once individuals are taught how to be curious rather than guilty when it comes to reflection, they regain control over consequences. The disappointment is converted into the energy of redesign through reflection.

Emotion should yield to structure in order to have reflection after failure. An obvious and replicable structure organizes what seems anarchy. This attitude is embodied in the three-step Analyze-Adjust-Apply process as below.

1. Analyze: Find out the contributing factors to the unwanted outcome. Was it bad planning, external restrictions, and misalignment of objectives or unrealistic time frames?
2. Adjust: Figure out what must be changed in terms of behaviors, tools or assumptions. What should you retain, abandon or initiate the next time?
3. Apply: Next attempt is applying the revised method as soon as possible. The repetition of testing averts reflection to theory.

This is a reflection of the scientific process: observe, hypothesize, experiment, and review. It turns failure into a personal loss and professional learning. The reflective individual does not perceive errors as evidence of incompetence but instead, as an experiment with some surprising results. Neff et al. (2005) argue that individuals who develop self-compassion in the face of failure are more motivated and are persistent since they view failures as learning and not a lack of ability. Self-kindness reflection creates strength; it substitutes clinical judgment with interest.

Figure 8.2: The 360 Degree Feedback

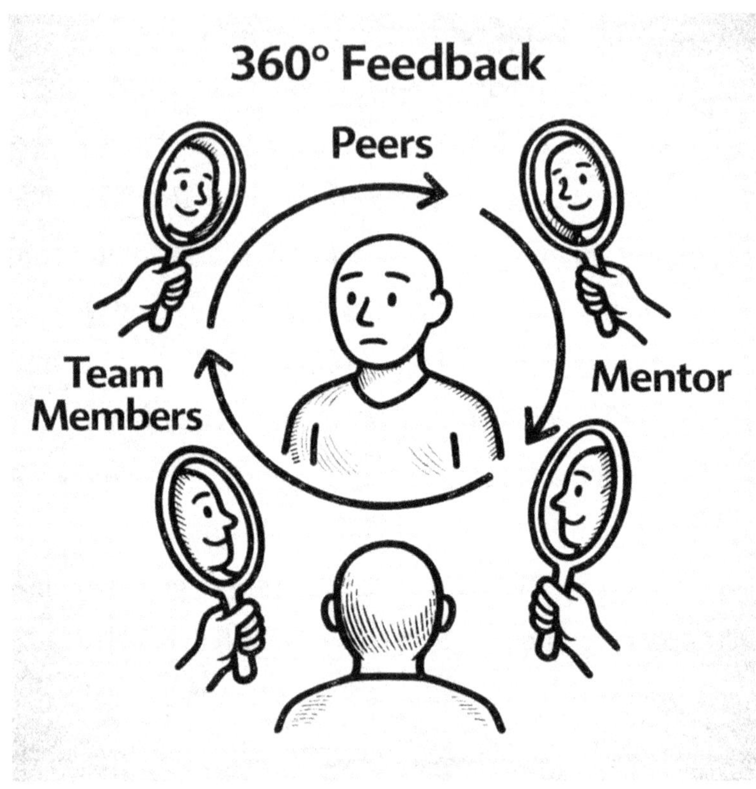

Figure 8.2 above shows the feedback loop of taking in- and assimilating- feedback. There are arrows depicted in the figure between self-review, peer feedback, and mentor insights, forming a complete circle of learning. It emphasizes that having a combination of personal reflection and external views is a whole circle of development and helps to identify blind spots, as well as to strengthen the responsibility to continuously improve them.

The process of reflection is enhanced by professional feedback. Positive feedbacks of friends, supervisors or customers make visible those patterns that one cannot see through his own experience. After-action reviews are a method that is used by numerous high-performing teams because it was originally developed in the U.S. Army, and other industries have since embraced it. This technique consists of four main questions:

1. What was intended?
2. What actually happened?
3. Why did it happen?
4. How shall we do it different next time?

These questions help people to turn abstract failure into quantifiable understanding by responding to their questions in a sincere manner. It is not a matter of blame-shifting but is a matter of truth collection. When leaders make reflective dialogue routine, then the teams will be learning laboratories and not fear arenas.

The same strategy can be effective in personal life. As supported by London and Smither (2002), when you fail to meet a fitness objective, have made a poor presentation, or wasted time, you need to write a failure story by giving yourself twenty minutes to do that. Record the chronology of events, find turning points, and get emotional triggers. Then enumerate the lessons learnt through this analysis. When these lessons are known, formulate a one-sentence action plan and start with the following words, "Next time I will." This little gesture turns a tale of guilt to that of development.

Figure 8.3: Dissecting Failure

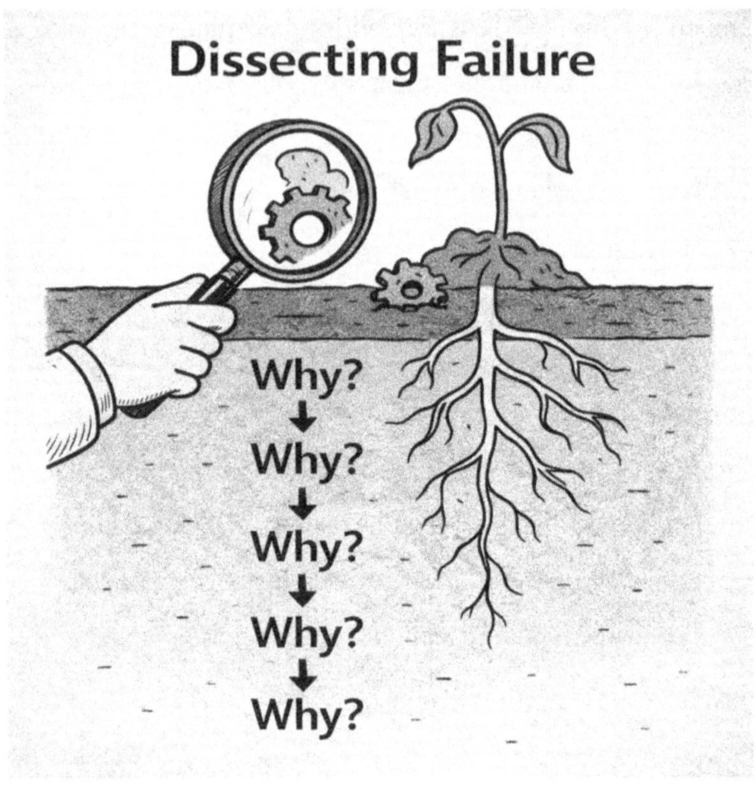

Figure 8.3 above describes the Analyze-Adjust-Apply model as a detection-diagnostic process cycle. The image demonstrates that reflection changes errors to fresh strategies. The arrows amongst the stages represent the momentum, as the next iteration produces finer insight, decreasing the frequency of errors and turning obstacles on the way to better output and advancements in work and innovative approaches and methods.

Reflecting on failure is not the need to experience pain again but it is about deriving wisdom. This is what is commonly referred to by psychologists as cognitive reappraisal, the capacity to redefine the negative experience in a positive way. As a strategic intervention, reappraisal disconnects shame and failure. It develops what could be referred to as emotional agility enabling one to get back on their feet faster and be more creative in facing the next challenge.

This is strengthened by self-compassion. It is a common misconception that mistreating oneself will inspire them to work harder but this is not the case as evidenced. Criticism of oneself is harsh and creates avoidance, whereas being kind creates persistence (Neff et al., 2005). Once reflection entails empathy, it is more likely that people will be ready to look at details truthfully and create enduring changes. Having a caring attitude will help us to view failure as a transient state, but not an identity.

Post failure reflection also enhances decision making. When examining the cause of the error, one will tend to discover incorrect assumptions or lack of information. As an example, when a project is not completed in time, it may turn out that there was lack of clarity in communication channels, or that priorities were different. Reflection is used to isolate the root cause instead of responding to superficial symptoms. Gradually, such a habit of analysis minimizes the errors.

On the organizational level, reflective leaders demonstrate a spirit of openness through modeling. This is because when managers publicly disclose their own errors and talk about what they have learnt they will reduce the overall fear of failure. Employees are more eager to experiment, thus innovation takes place. Conversely, punitive cultures result in silence and silence kills development. The same fact is true of people: when you treat yourself as an experimenter, and not an accused, learning speed increases.

In order to make the process of reflection adjustment sustainable, develop a systematic rhythm. Create short debriefs on the schedule with projects, exams or individual milestones. Use a special improvement journal of three columns: Situation, Lesson and Next Action. The notes show improvement over months and they help avoid making the same errors. Every page goes to show that development is cumulative-that what seemed to have been a failure has been experience.

It takes humility, patience and courage to learn out of failure. Humility chooses to be less than perfect; patient has time to make changes; braveness confronts the truth without any excuse. Under these circumstances, disappointment is turned into direction when these qualities are combined together.

Failure, considered in the context of reflection, is the most sincere system of feedback to use. It is a more effective lesson than success can be in that it requires cognition and adjustment. Any failure is a dress rehearsal to perfection. Yesterday, at the time it is carefully analyzed, and acted upon with rapidity, today becomes tomorrow.

8.3 Celebrating Small Wins and Staying Motivated

Reflection is a process and a practice of not only diagnosing but also appreciating. Although reflection shows what should be better, it also shows the areas that have already become better. Praising the ground even when the achievements are minor feeds the drive necessary to continue onwards. Amabile and Kramer (2011) believe that individuals become more engaged and feel better when they recognize the progressive accomplishment of significant objectives, which they refer to as the progress principle. Every little success serves as an indication that you are fighting, and big dreams can be turned into small achievements.

Small victories are important since the human brain is a reward-feedback mechanism. Every recognition of progress causes the release of positive emotion, which supports continuity. According to Woolley and Fishbach (2016), instant rewards allow maintaining motivation in long projects since they generate pleasure in effort itself, rather than in the end of these efforts. People are more inclined to complete what they have initiated when they feel rewarded and at the same time, they are pursuing something.

However, it is not revelry, but tact. It changes criticism to rejuvenation. The individual preventing to pay attention to improvement enhances self-confidence and burnout. The achievement is self-generative, as all the acknowledgements of the improvement feed the need to go further.

Figure 8.4: Adapt and Grow

Figure 8.4 above describes adaptive learning as a cyclic process. In the figure, there is a curved arrow between feedback and the confidence. With each iteration, there is increased strength. It shows that understanding small gains followed by applying lessons makes one more resilient. The grouping of progress does not take a linear form but the form of upward loops which represent sustained growth via constant adaptation and support.

The issue of generosity does not concern rewarding. We find ourselves doing no more than the bare minimum to enjoy a good party: a superficial check-up on the self, an agreeable smile or a chance to put down a victory and transition to the next activity. The micro-celebrations help to make the spirits stay in goals without distraction. One of the last minute activities of a teacher can be called writing one sentence on a lesson which was not as bad as it has been initially perceived.

As an example, it becomes calm when a nurse finds some time to record his/her experience with a patient which has been already identified to result in being stressed. A team leader can start a team meeting by stating one of the latest achievements and go on to the obstacles. All these are the steps of rebranding as a sign of improvement, and transforming the perception of the performance of people.

Motivation dies at the time when reflection is directed to gaps. People get to identify work with inadequacy as opposed to progress. A reflection process is balanced and incorporates an acknowledgement of what has been done well as well as appreciation of what was learned. The practice of appreciation does not only keep the energy alive, but also self-belief. Self-recognition in the long run turns out to be armor against discouragement, guarding long-term plans against temporary disappointments.

Figure 8.5: Celebrate Small Wins

Figure 8.5 above shows little victories piling like stepping stones, climbing up. One of the stones is engraved with a small success, delivery of a task, better concentration, and new ability. The image is that the motivation to support small successes with repeated observations doubles the effect, making single actions give rise to a wave of dynamism and strength.

Organized partying can change culture in workplaces. Some organizations have the so called success boards or weekly highlight email as employees write one big or little achievement. These ceremonies bring collective optimism, which enhances motivation and identification. Collaboration and reduced stress in teams that share in the celebration of progress are reported to be stronger and less competitive due to the feeling of communal success as opposed to competition.

At the individual level, the same could be performed by a wins journal. Documenting at least three little accomplishments in a day such as doing a workout, being good at time management, solving a tough talk, creates evidence of being competent. Looking back at these entries following a long week is a factual way of reminding myself that progress is occurring, even when it does not seem to. The habit nurtures appreciation, and the latter makes one more resilient and joyful.

The values of gratitude and recognition also contribute to grit, which is the long-term interest and commitment to goals by psychologists. Duckworth et al. (2007) discovered that gritty people persist in failures in their quest to get ahead since they are able to see a sense in improvement as opposed to perfection. Making a big deal out of small achievements, the latter refill emotional resources and keep them committed despite the remote end results. The fact is that every recognition of progress is a little deposit in the emotional bank that invests the persistence.

Small wins are another way of recalibration. Having people record success is a frequent occurrence and as a result achievable goals that were initially felt to be too ambitious come into reach. The mind ceases to count success by the mere completion and instead learns to appreciate consistency. This change decreases the procrastination because individuals feel satisfied with the progress and not the end product.

Congratulation and contemplation constitute a full motivational cycle. Lessons are found in reflection and learning in celebration. They collectively achieve sustainable productivity which is not driven by pressure but positive momentum. The contemplative individual who adores as well as studies makes him student and teacher: deconstructing, modifying, praising, and then, progressing.

In order to make celebration a routine practice, make it a part of your reflection habits. Having addressed the standard reflection questions: What went well? What can be better? And what am I proud of to-day? The solution does not have to be big. Persistence is pride and achievement is pride. Recording the number of pride daily you train the mind to go out to improve and pursue joy at the same time.

Celebration leaders help teams to appreciate improvement. When a manager acknowledges the creative concept or the small step of an employee, it is an indication that development is observed and appreciated. This creates mental security and internal drive. Identifying effort in classrooms, in addition to outcome, motivates students to make intellectual risks. In any setting, celebration is the emotional equivalent of analysis; it makes the learning process human and optimistic.

Small wins do not imply to disregard any mistakes; instead, it is putting them in a moderate perspective of progress. The reflecting glass of identifying mistakes must identify initiative as well. As time goes by, this balance prevents ambition to become exhaustion. Progress has ceased to be an attempt to move toward a far-off achievement but a beat of footsteps- one footstep to the next-one footstep that has been made, one footstep that is prized.

The lifelong journeys get so discouraging when one is not known. Celebration restores it. A smile at a small achievement, a word in a journal, and a word in acknowledgment of hard work which may seem as trivial, may go along with the goal. Combined with an honest sense of self-reflection, one can create a process of development that can be implemented over a long period: learn, change, celebrate, and repeat.

8.4 Continuous Improvement through Reflection

Constant renewal is the very meaning of real efficiency. Reflection will make sure that improvement is not accidental but is carried out through deliberate, cyclical processes of learning. Once individuals consider growth as a constant process and not a single accomplishment, they create room in which progress becomes a way of living. The trick that transforms a habitual performance into a constant idealization is reflection- every analysis is a new trial; every change an improvement of performance.

The Plan-Do-Check-Act (PDCA) model represents this philosophy, the initial model designed by W. Edwards Deming, which is currently used extensively in organizational and personal development (Imai, 2012). The model reflects the ethos of the never-ending consideration in four steps that are simple and yet effective:

1. Plan: Develop a strategy, a goal, a habit that should be improved.
2. Do: Implement it regularly within a period of time.

3. Check: Reflect on results- see what was effective and what was not.

4. Act: Revise the plan based on lessons learned, and restart afresh.

These are not linear but the steps make a learning loop. Every cycle enhances the knowledge and decision-making. Be it the process of developing a large company or the daily routine in the morning, PDCA captures the cycle of development: strategic planning, conscious experimentation, sincere reflection, and responsive adjustment.

Figure 8.6: Progress Dashboard

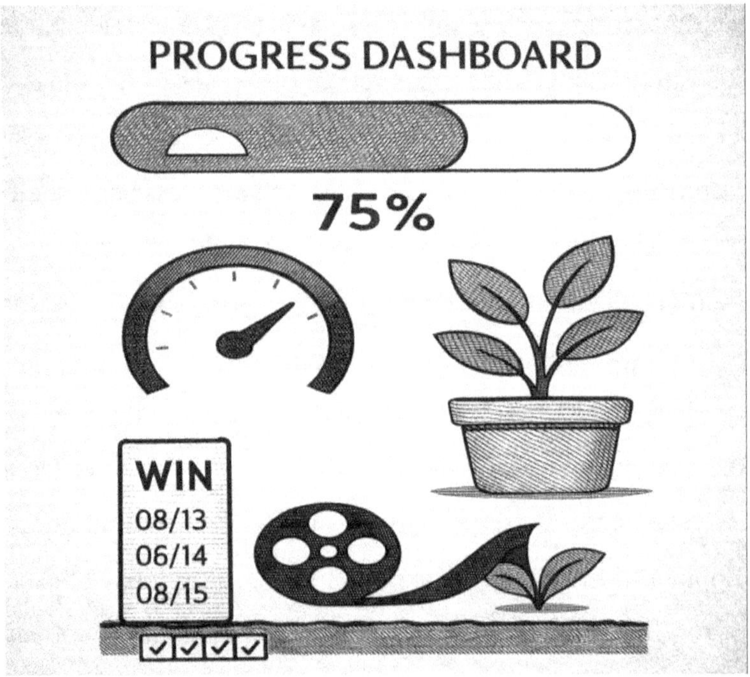

Figure 8.6 shows how the metrics of reflection can be represented using a personal dashboard. The figure depicts the

trends of habits, mood swings, and the output graphs over time. It highlights that self-tracking is only significant when one views it in a reflective way and transforms raw data into wisdom. The dashboard itself represents the consciousness as something on the move; improvement that has been noted, cognized, and continually perfected.

The current technology has simplified self-reflection to be quantified. Since the inception of fitness trackers to productivity apps, now people can see their behavior trends with a high degree of accuracy. Statistics of actions, work time, or sleep are all in favor of development. However, as Gouveia et al. (2015) found, measurement alone seldom produces behavior change. Data can only be truly transformed when it is matched with meaning, when numbers are made stories. Reflection offers such interpretation. Digital tracking can easily turn into noise; it can also be a mirror of technology.

In order to implement PDCA individually, start with something small. Select a habit, such as enhancing the quality of sleep, limiting distractions, or writing regularly.

- Plan: Have a goal, for example, sleep by 10.30 pm for five nights a week.
- Do: Adhere to the routine in two weeks with observing the conditions that influence success.
- Check: Research the results in good faith. Did bedtime improve? What interfered?

- Act: Change behavior- cut back on screen time before sleep or schedule reminders earlier.

The repetition of this process makes reflection a day to day experiment of science. Every practice develops towards mastery. Eventually, the cycle starts to become the second law, a psychological process of trial and error, learning, and adapting.

Constant reflection is anti-complacency. What was successful yesterday might not be successful today. The situation changes, industries develop and priorities grow. Habits that were working at one time can slip out of sight without being reviewed by one regularly. Routine reflection: monthly, quarterly, annually, etc. It assists people to stay on track with the changing objectives rather than sailing on previously held presumptions.

Figure 8.7: Continuous Improvement Loop

The PDCA model in figure 8.7 above demonstrates that the process of personal development is a looping process of acting and reflecting. Used extensively in both corporate and personal development models, the PDCA (Plan–Do Check Act) cycle makes lasting behavior change effective (with periodic review and corrective action embedded).

Companies that adopt this have a learning orientation. According to Senge (2010), organizations that manage to survive in changing environments develop the capacity to reflect as a group and change systems according to the feedbacks. The same is true on an individual basis. When one makes oneself a learning system, i.e.

reviewing and refining as opposed to defending old habits, the individual remains adaptive to change.

It is also through constant thinking that ambition and realism are balanced. The external reviewer is able to notice when objectives are becoming too detached to values or when work is taking up more than it is giving back. A quarterly review is similar to internal audit: it helps to ensure that time and energy is spent in the appropriate direction. During such a review, ask the following.

- Do my actions correspond to what is really important?
- Which jobs create growth, and which are just motion preserving jobs?
- What can I cease, initiate or redesign to get nearer to my vision?

These questions make reflection strategic renewal. Every response focuses the energies to positive cause. Humility is also enhanced through reflection-based improvement. An individual who is dedicated to lifelong learning should embrace the aspect of "being flawed" as "being here to stay." One can always go deeper to a new level of refining; of trying to be more insightful. Such an attitude substitutes frustration with curiosity; every challenge turns into an invitation to learn instead of the evidence of incompetence.

Continuous improvement does not mean perpetual efforts but balanced improvement. Reflection makes sure that the growth is done not drained but consciously. These steps, plan, do, check and act, provide rhythm and reprieve - work, and then learn, learn, refine. The PDCA cycle is like a heartbeat and sustains growth by means of constant repetition.

To make continuous improvement an institution, make review meetings with yourself. Establish time limits, e.g. at the end of each quarter, to determine consistency between action and plan. Record important conclusions, learning points, and potential improvements. Nobody is going to tell you what your goals revitalized you and what exhausted you. Whenever a task takes time but not serving long-term purpose, redesign it, delegate it or eliminate it. The reflection in this manner turns out to be the upkeep program of the intentional existence.

Flexibility is the best advantage of constant reflection. Life does not usually run as expected. Things evolve, demands vary and new perilous challenges emerge. The reflective individual experiences these changes with grace since he or she is constantly changing direction never being dedicated to a single notion of success. They realize that it is not an event, but it is a constant dialogue between effort and awareness to make improvements.

Action without reflection and reflection without action are pathways to burnout and stagnation, respectively. Reflection is a constant way of enhancing that brings together both sides of the equation. It makes learning dynamic and movement significant. The key to sustainable growth is in this loop: not doing more, but knowing better each day.

8.5 Real-Life Scenario: From Burnout to Balance

Maria is a Nairobi nurse in the critical-care unit and once thought that efficiency was a state of being in constant motion. Her days started earlier than the sunrise and ended late in the night. She missed lunch breaks, disregarded the concept of exhaustion and discounted the idea of rest as a weakness. Maria has been associating busyness with commitment. She quantified her worth in terms of the number of hours she worked and the number of tasks she accomplished. Patients were impressed by her dedication and supervisors delighted in her expediency, but deep within her she could feel the gradual drain of vivacity. What had started as a love affair over care had become fatigue masquerading itself as being productive.

All this changed one evening when she was in a hospital workshop on reflective practice. The session covered the role of reflection in assisting healthcare workers to manage stress and enhance clinical judgment. One thought came to her with a force that could be called the thought of the possibility of being faster by being slower in the long run. That evening Maria purchased a small notebook and put it into her uniform pocket. It would become her "mirror."

She wrote three lines each day, before leaving the ward:

1. What went well today?
2. What felt difficult?
3. What will I adjust tomorrow?

At first, it felt awkward. The reflection habit appeared to be luxurious as other people were hurrying to get home by bus. But in two weeks there were patterns out of those simple notes. She observed that her energy was at its highest during the period between 8:00 a.m. and 11:00 a.m. and then it dropped drastically after lunch. She noticed that she was planning her most complicated activities, such as medication calculations and patient documentation, at the time of the lowest concentration. She was less fatigued because of changing to do such things earlier in the day and having a ten-minute walk before afternoon rounds to make her more concentrated and full of energy.

Much was not lost before her colleagues found out the difference. As a result of this, Maria was calmer, made fewer mistakes and began passing in reports on time. When I asked her what had changed she responded and said that she began to think and then she acted. She got motivated and informed her new direction to her staff. They began to make brief micro-reflections at the end of each shift collectively. They were standing in a circle around the nurse station and took sixty seconds to respond to one question aloud: What did we learn today?

These mini debriefings changed the team dynamic. Nurses did not leave the ward feeling frustrated or drained as they rushed out the door, but rather they felt a sense of completion and purpose. They would talk about small achievements, such as managing a patient-patient interaction without losing their temper, or record small lessons, such as rearranging the medication trolley so that it will be easier to reach. In the long run, morale was enhanced, and mistakes reduced. Reflection, which was initially an individual practice, was transformed into a group learning practice.

Maria also realized that speculation was not a preserve of academicians or administrators- speculation was a survival strategy. Her cell-phone was her friend and she had a notebook as her guide and counselor. She would do the processing of errors instead of pushing them down on the hard days when the errors were too numerous. When everything went well, she wrote thankfulness which enhanced a sense of success. Gradually, the process of reflection changed her identity, as a professional nurse who works too much, to a thinking person.

She understood that some thinking increased her performance and it reinstated her sense of balance. She managed to get back to what she was at her job prior to performing her duties not to compete but to assist people. The reflection practice helped her to become less anxious and more present with patients. Her colleagues said that she was more relaxed and focused. Maria herself was rejuvenated and found joy in minor things, such as a smile of a patient who was recovering or a teamwork that was successful.

The change in Maria is similar to the results of Sirois (2014), who indicated that people with a reflective time orientation (those who take time to reflect on past events before taking action) are less stressed and less prone to procrastination. Reflection enhances emotional control and decision-making forming a consistent balance between work and rest. To Maria, reflection did not involve over-thinking the past but rather planning well on what to do next.

In a few months, the cogitation reconstituted her days. She began planning her week in a goal-orientated tone: she created a Monday planning, a Friday review, and end of shift brief notes. She was made to identify the first signs of exhaustion and to delegate. She never looked at rest as time with wasted no purpose, but as an investment in better care. She also found equilibrium even in the hospital. She applied the same reflective practice to her personal life- she kept a journal about when she was grateful at home and she altered the family habit and she set realistic boundaries between her working and rest.

Reflection turned out to be the silent self-leadership of Maria. Through her behaviors and results, she started to foresee difficulties before they grew out of proportion. Maria taught her the same habit when a new nurse joined her team. The two of them perfected the micro-reflection process and included a whiteboard next to the station called What We Learned Today. The board was soon full of brief observations and inspirational quotes, as a group development mirror.

Maria's narrative shows that reflection is not about perfection but about connection: connection with oneself, connection with values and connection with others. Maria discovered through reflection that acceleration does not make things truly efficient but alignment does. She started moving slowly on purpose, and this is how she started to move forward with clarity and purpose.

Reflection enabled her to maintain her career in a stressful profession in the long run. Where others had flamed out, she had made strength out of consciousness. Reflection became her day-to-day renewal practice, a psychological balance point between the state of disorganization and order. What started as a notebook exercise turned out to be a cultural change in her ward and a new meaning of success.

It is illustrated in the experience of Maria that depicts the universal power of reflection. The point is that there are no differences concerning the sphere of healthcare, education, or business as the same rule can be said that taking a moment and thinking can multiply the value of action by 2. Meditation will change the exhaustion to enlightenment, the mistakes to experience and the practice to the excellence. Her experience indicates that the easiest and surest way to be back on track even in the most challenging conditions is by reflection.

8.6 Chapter Summary

Efficiency is sustainable upon reflection. It converts ordinary life into learning which is systematic; it converts failure into mastery, and ordinary success into growth process which is long lasting. One of the things that reflection teaches people is the need to pause and take a moment, critically assess, and put back on track. It is a science of consciousness which transforms work into development and action into knowing.

A reflective individual is not arrogant but tactical; never satisfied. Through introspection, one gets to know how to find patterns, hone habits, and what actually makes things work. Reflection makes motion directionless, and turns productivity, the measure of speed, into the measure of wisdom.

Self-assessment on a regular basis enhances decision-making and uncovers the strengths and weaknesses. Failures are transformed into feedback and analyzed and adapted when they fail, and not seen as a loss. Self-compassion substitutes self-criticism and transforms failures into useful information to succeed in the future.

Reflective praise should be used to celebrate small successes in order to maintain the motivation and high spirit. The quality of viewing growth as a process of small increments adds onto the perseverance and supports the belief that growth takes place in small steps and consciously.

The secret of continual improvement is repetition. The Plan-Do-Check-Act model reflects the process of thoughts, purposeful planning, sounding action, results analysis and positive feedback to the next action.

Lastly, reflection is a moderating variable. This protects against burnout because it will reconnect action and meaning as well as ambition and self-care. Spirit is brought back into a world where everybody is obsessed with speed. It also ensures that success is achieved but is also understood, sustained and justified.

This Week's Five-Step Reflection Challenge

1. Establish a Daily Mirror Time: Ten minutes nightly: Respond to what went well? What can I adjust?"
2. Write One Failure Narrative: Use this method to describe a recent failure, learn, and plan one behavior change.
3. Record Three Wins: Keep a record of three little successes a day to keep the motivation in the right direction.
4. Organize a Weekly Review: Select an hour this weekday to analyze the goals in terms of the PDCA format.
5. Share Reflection with a Peer: Share reflections with a friend or colleague to become accountable and to gain a new lens.

References

Aeon, B., Faber, A., & Panaccio, A. (2021). Does time management work? A meta-analysis. *Academy of Management Perspectives, 35*(4), 602–628. https://doi.org/10.1371/journal.pone.0245066

Adiga, U. (2023). Enhancing occupational health and ergonomics for optimal workplace well-being: A review. *International Journal of Chemical and Biochemical Sciences*, *24*(4), 157-164.

Albulescu, P., Macsinga, I., Rusu, A., Sulea, C., Bodnaru, A., & Tulbure, B. T. (2022). " Give me a break!" A systematic review and meta-analysis on the efficacy of micro-breaks for increasing well-being and performance. *Plos One*, *17*(8). https://doi.org/10.1371/journal.pone.0272460

Allen, D. (2015). *Getting things done: The art of stress-free productivity.* Penguin.

Amabile, T. M., & Kramer, S. J. (2011). *The progress principle: Using small wins to ignite joy, engagement, and creativity at work.* Harvard Business Review Press.

Artazcoz, L., Cortès, I., Escribà-Agüir, V., Bartoll, X., Basart, H., & Borrell, C. (2013). Long working hours and health status among employees in Europe: between-country differences. *Scandinavian Journal of Work, Environment & Health*, 369-378. https://doi.org/10.5271/sjweh.3333

Bakker, A. B., & Demerouti, E. (2017). Job demands–resources theory: Taking stock and looking forward. *Journal of*

Occupational Health Psychology, 22(3), 273–285. http://dx.doi.org/10.1037/ocp0000056

Baumeister, R. F., & Heatherton, T. F. (1996). Self-regulation and performance. *Psychological Inquiry, 31*(2).

Belbin, R. M. (2012). *Management teams: Why they succeed or fail.* Routledge. https://doi.org/10.1108/hrmid.2011.04419cae.002

Boyatzis, R. E., Goleman, D., & Rhee, K. (2000). Clustering competence in emotional intelligence: Insights from the Emotional Competence Inventory (ECI). *Handbook of emotional intelligence*, *99*(6).

Charness, G., Le Bihan, Y., &Villeval, M. C. (2024). Mindfulness training, cognitive performance and stress reduction. *Journal of Economic Behavior & Organization*, *217*, 207-226. https://doi.org/10.1016/j.jebo.2023.10.027

Cirillo, F. (2018). *The Pomodoro technique: The acclaimed time-management system that has transformed how we work.* Crown Currency. https://www.flowloop.io/download/pomodorotechnique.pdf

Claessens, B. J., Van Eerde, W., Rutte, C. G., & Roe, R. A. (2007). A review of the time management literature. *Personnel Review*, *36*(2), 255-276. https://www.emerald.com/insight/content/doi/10.1108/00483480710726136/full/html

Clear, J. (2018). *Atomic habits: An easy & proven way to build good habits & break bad ones*. Penguin.

Covey, S. R. (2020). *The 7 habits of highly effective people (30th anniversary edition).* Simon & Schuster.

Creswell, J. D. (2017). Mindfulness interventions. *Annual Review of Psychology*, *68*(2017). https://r.jordan.im/download/mindfulness/creswell2017.pdf

Cross, R., Davenport, T. H., & Gray, P. (2019). Collaborate smarter, not harder. *MIT Sloan Management Review*, *61*(1). https://sloanreview.mit.edu/article/collaborate-smarter-not-harder/

Csikszentmihalyi, M. (1990). *Flow: The psychology of optimal experience.* Harper & Row.

Di Stefano, G., Gino, F., Pisano, G. P., & Staats, B. R. (2014). Learning by thinking: How reflection aids performance. *Academy of Management Proceedings*, 1–47. https://larryferlazzo.edublogs.org/files/2013/08/reflection-1di0i76.pdf

Drucker, P. F. (2006). *The effective executive: The definitive guide to getting the right things done*. Harper & Row.

Duckworth, A. L., Peterson, C., Matthews, M. D., & Kelly, D. R. (2007). Grit: perseverance and passion for long-term goals. *Journal of Personality and Social Psychology*, *92*(6), 1087.

Duckworth, A. L., & Seligman, M. E. P. (2017). The science and practice of self-control. *Perspectives on Psychological*

Science: A Journal of the Association for Psychological Science, *12*(5), 715–718. https://doi.org/10.1177/1745691617690880

Dweck, C. (2006). *Mindset: Changing the way you think to fulfil your potential.* Random House.

Dweck, C. S. (2016). *Mindset: The new psychology of success.* Random House.

Edmondson, A. C. (2011). Strategies for learning from failure. *Harvard Business Review*, *89*(4), 48- 55.

Epstein, R. M., & Krasner, M. S. (2013). Physician resilience: What it means, why it matters, and how to promote it. *Academic Medicine*, *88*(3), 301-303.

Eshiett, I. O., & Eshiett, O. E. (2025). Employee motivation and sustainable productivity assessment in automated work environment. *Journal of Comprehensive Business Administration Research*. https://doi.org/10.47852/bonviewJCBAR52024223

Freund, A. M., & Hennecke, M. (2015). On means and ends: The role of goal focus in successful goal pursuit. *Current Directions in Psychological Science*, *24*(2). https://www.researchgate.net/publication/275221807_On_Means_and_Ends_The_Role_of_Goal_Focus_in_Successful_Goal_Pursuit

Frontzkowski, Y., Krick, A., & Felfe, J. (2025). Harder, better, faster, but more fatigued: The impact of multitasking on videoconferences, performance and fatigue. *Computers in*

Human Behavior Reports. https://doi.org/10.1016/j.chbr.2025.100736

George, M. L. (2006). *Lean Six Sigma: Combining Six Sigma Qualitywith Lean Production Speed.* McGraw-Hill.

Gollwitzer, P. M., & Sheeran, P. (2006). Implementation intentions and goal achievement: A meta-analysis of effects and processes. *Advances in Experimental Social Psychology*, *38*. https://kops.uni-konstanz.de/server/api/core/bitstreams/d4f710b4-a505-49ef-a831-5b8d7675100b/content

Gouveia, R., Karapanos, E., & Hassenzahl, M. (2015, September). How do we engage with activity trackers? A longitudinal study of Habito. In *Proceedings of the 2015 ACM International Joint Conference on Pervasive and Ubiquitous Computing*. http://dx.doi.org/10.1145/2750858.2804290

Grant, A. M., & Parker, S. K. (2009). 7 redesigning work design theories: The rise of relational and proactive perspectives. *Academy of Management annals*, *3*(1). https://journals.aom.org/doi/abs/10.5465/19416520903047327

Grant, A. M., & Shandell, M. S. (2022). Social motivation at work: The organizational psychology of effort for, against, and with others. *Annual Review of Psychology*, *73*(1), 301-326. https://doi.org/10.1146/annurev-psych-060321-033406

Harkin, B., Webb, T. L., Chang, B. P., Prestwich, A., Conner, M., Kellar, I., ...& Sheeran, P. (2016). Does monitoring goal progress promote goal attainment? A meta-analysis of the experimental evidence. *Psychological Bulletin*, *142*(2). http://dx.doi.org/10.1037/bul0000025

Heatherton, T. F. (2011). Neuroscience of self and self-regulation. *Annual Review of Psychology*, *62*(1). https://pmc.ncbi.nlm.nih.gov/articles/PMC3056504/pdf/nihms245639.pdf

Hoffman, E. K. (2017). Grit: The power of passion and perseverance. *Growth: The Journal of the Association for Christians in Student Development*, *16*(16), 8. https://pillars.taylor.edu/cgi/viewcontent.cgi?article=1149&context=acsd_growth

Hofstede, G. (2011). Dimensionalizingcultures: The Hofstede Model in context. *OnlineReadings in Psychology and Culture*, 2(1). https://doi.org/10.9707/2307-0919.1014

Huang, M. H., & Rust, R. T. (2021). A strategic framework for artificial intelligence in marketing.*Journal of the Academy of Marketing Science, 49*(1), 30–50. https://doi.org/10.1007/s11747-020-00749-9

Hughes, L., Mavi, R. K., Aghajani, M., Fitzpatrick, K., Gunaratnege, S. M., Shekarabi, S. A. H., ... & Dwivedi, Y. K. (2025). Impact of artificial intelligence on project management (PM): Multi-expert perspectives on advancing knowledge and driving innovation toward

PM2030. *Journal of Innovation & Knowledge, 10*(5). https://doi.org/10.1016/j.jik.2025.100772

Imai, M. (2012). Gemba Kaizen: A commonsense approach to a continuous improvement strategy second edition.

Institute of Education Science (2022). Growth mindset interventions: Intervention Report | Supporting Postsecondary Success. https://ies.ed.gov/ncee/wwc/Docs/InterventionReports/WWC_GrowthMindset_IR_report.pdf

International Labour Organization (2022). *Working time and work-life balance around the world.* ILO Publications. https://www.ilo.org/sites/default/files/wcmsp5/groups/public/%40ed_protect/%40protrav/%40travail/documents/publication/wcms_864222.pdf

Inzlicht, M., Shenhav, A., & Olivola, C. Y. (2018). The effort paradox: Effort is both costly and valued. *Trends in Cognitive Sciences*, *22*(4). http://doi:10.1016/j.tics.2018.01.007

Jena, L. K., & Basu, E. (2018). Deep work: Rules for focused success in a distracted world. *Vikalpa: The Journal for Decision Makers*, *43*(1), 58-60. https://doi.org/10.1177/0256090917753047

Koch, R. (2011). *The 80/20 principle: The secret to achieving more with less.* Crown Business.

Koch, I., Poljac, E., Müller, H., &Kiesel, A. (2018). Cognitive structure, flexibility, and plasticity in human multitasking—An integrative review of dual-task and task-switching research. *Psychological Bulletin*, *144*(6). http://dx.doi.org/10.1037/bul0000144

Koundal, N., Abdalhadi, A., Al-Quraishi, M. S., Elamvazuthi, I., Moosavi, M. S., Guillet, C., ...& Saad, N. M. (2024). Effect of interruptions and cognitive demand on mental workload: A critical review. *IEEE Access*, *12*. https://hal.science/hal-04563076v1/file/LISPEN_ACCESS_2024_MOOSAVI.pdf

Kruk, M. E., Gage, A. D., Arsenault, C., Jordan, K., Leslie, H. H., Roder-DeWan, S., Adeyi, O., Barker, P., Daelmans, B., Doubova, S. V., English, M., García-Elorrio, E., Guanais, F., Gureje, O., Hirschhorn, L. R., Jiang, L., Kelley, E., Lemango, E. T., Liljestrand, J., Malata, A., … Pate, M. (2018). High-quality health systems in the sustainable development goals era: Time for a revolution. *The Lancet. Global Health*, *6*(11), e1196–e1252. https://doi.org/10.1016/S2214-109X(18)30386-3

Kuhnel, J., Bledow, R., & Kuonath, A. (2023). Overcoming procrastination: Time pressure and positive affect as compensatory routes to action. *Journal of Business and Psychology*, *38*(4), 803-819. https://doi.org/10.1007/s10869-022-09817-z

Kushlev, K., & Dunn, E. W. (2015). Checking email less frequently reduces stress. *Computers in Human Behavior*, *43*, 220-228. http://dx.doi.org/10.1016/j.chb.2014.11.005

Lim, W. M. (2023). The workforce revolution: Reimagining work, workers, and workplaces for the future. *Global Business and Organizational Excellence*, *42*(4), 5-10. https://onlinelibrary.wiley.com/doi/pdf/10.1002/joe.22218

Locke, E. A., & Latham, G. P. (2019). The development of goal setting theory: A half-century retrospective. *Motivation Science, 5*(2), 93–105. http://dx.doi.org/10.1037/mot0000127

London, M., & Smither, J. W. (2002). Feedback orientation, feedback culture, and the longitudinal performance management process. *Human Resource Management Review*, *12*(1), 81-100.

Mackey, M. (2024). Ergonomic design. In *Routledge Handbook of High-Performance Workplaces* (pp. 36-51). Routledge.

Mark, G., Gudith, D., & Klocke, U. (2008, April). The cost of interrupted work: More speed and stress. In *Proceedings of the SIGCHI Conference on Human Factors in Computing Systems* (pp. 107-110). https://interruptions.net/literature/Mark-CHI08.pdf

Mazmanian, M., Orlikowski, W. J., & Yates, J. (2013). The autonomy paradox: The implications of mobile email devices for knowledge professionals.*Organization Science*, 24(5). http://dx.doi.org/10.1287/orsc.1120.0806

McGonigal, K. (2013). *The willpower instinct: How self-control works, why it matters, and what you can do to get more of it*. Penguin.https://static10.labirint.ru/books/330517/demo.pdf

Mesman, E., Vreeker, A., & Hillegers, M. (2021). Resilience and mental health in children and adolescents: an update of the recent literature and future directions. *Current Opinion in Psychiatry*, *34*(6), 586–592. https://doi.org/10.1097/YCO.0000000000000741

Miller, T. (2020, December 17). 'The unexamined life is not worth living' — Socrates: Socrates's quote inspires writers to keep writing. *The Brave Writer*. https://medium.com/the-brave-writer/the-unexamined-life-is-not-worth-living-e90573573e8f

Miyake, A., & Friedman, N. P. (2012). The nature and organization of individual differences in executive functions: Four general conclusions. *Current Directions in Psychological Science*, *21*(1), 8-14. https://journals.sagepub.com/doi/abs/10.1177/0963721411429458

Moffitt, T. E., Arseneault, L., Belsky, D., Dickson, N., Hancox, R. J., Harrington, H., ...& Caspi, A. (2011). A gradient of childhood self-control predicts health, wealth, and public safety. *Proceedings of the National Academy of Sciences*, *108*(7). https://doi.org/10.1073/pnas.1010076108

Neff, K. D., Hsieh, Y. P., & Dejitterat, K. (2005). Self-compassion, achievement goals, and coping with academic failure. *Self and Identity*, *4*(3), 263-287.

Nonaka, I., & Takeuchi, H. (2019). *The wise company: How companies create continuous innovation.* Oxford University Press. https://dokumen.live/reviews/s4CIJ1/245401/4988550-the-wise-company-how-companies-create-continuous-i

Oettingen, G., & Gollwitzer, P. M. (2010). Strategies of setting and implementing goals: Mental contrasting and implementation intentions. https://kops.uni-konstanz.de/server/api/core/bitstreams/f312f6c1-116d-496b-9706-ee8a91e616ac/content

Ohly, S., & Bastin, L. (2023). Effects of task interruptions caused by notifications from communication applications on strain and performance. *Journal of Occupational Health*, *65*(1), e12408. https://doi.org/10.1002/1348-9585.12408

Ohno, T. (2019). *Toyota production system: Beyond large-scale production.* Routledge.

Oymirzayeva, M., & Murtozayeva, Z. (2024). How to build good habits and break bad ones in James Clear's "Atomic Habits". *News of UzMUjournal* , *1* (1.3), 1. https://pdfs.semanticscholar.org/37dd/4574638b6f02943911c53fd02162e3fb5ac6.pdf

Parke, M. R., Weinhardt, J. M., Brodsky, A., Tangirala, S., & DeVoc, S. E. (2018). When daily planning improves employee performance: The importance of planning type, engagement, and interruptions. *Journal of Applied Psychology*, *103*(3). https://doi.org/10.1037/apl0000278

Perez, J. (2014). *Focus: The hidden driver of excellence [review] /Goleman, Daniel.* HarperCollins. https://digitalcommons.andrews.edu/cgi/viewcontent.cgi?article=1237&context=jacl

Perinchery, N. (2023). A gender study on self-comparison, self-compassion and self-improvement motivation among young adults. *International Journal of Interdisciplinary Approaches in Psychology*, *1*(1), 50-66.

Posner, M. I., & Rothbart, M. K. (1998). Attention, self-regulation, and consciousness. *Philosophical Transactions of the Royal Society B, 373*(1756). https://pmc.ncbi.nlm.nih.gov/articles/PMC1692414/pdf/9854264.pdf

Raichle, M. E., & Gusnard, D. A. (2002). Appraising the brain's energy budget. *Proceedings of the National Academy of Sciences of the United States of America*, *99*(16), 10237–10239. https://doi.org/10.1073/pnas.172399499

Rigby, D. K., Sutherland, J., & Noble, A. (2018). *Agile at scale.* Harvard Business Review. https://todopmp.com/wp-content/uploads/2018/12/agile-at-scale.pdf

Robertson, M. M., Ciriello, V. M., & Garabet, A. M. (2013). Office ergonomics training and a sit-stand workstation: Effects on musculoskeletal and visual symptoms and performance of office workers. *Applied Ergonomics*, *44*(1), 73–85. https://doi.org/10.1016/j.apergo.2012.05.001

Rubinstein, J. S., Meyer, D. E., & Evans, J. E. (2001). Executive control of cognitive processes in task switching. *Journal of Experimental Psychology: Human Perception and Performance*, *27*(4). https://www.apa.org/pubs/journals/releases/xhp274763.pdf

Schwartz, T., & McCarthy, C. (2007). Manage your energy, not your time. *Harvard Business Review, 85*(10). https://wendyjocum.com.au/wp-content/uploads/2014/02/Time-Mgt-Manage-your-Energy-Not-your-Time-HO-8-v1.pdf

Seryapina, Y. S. (2018). The concept of "readiness for pedagogical activity": motivational readiness, psychological readiness, readiness to innovative activity, *10*(4), 77-86.

Sirois, F. M. (2014). Out of sight, out of time? A meta–analytic investigation of procrastination and time perspective. *European Journal of Personality*, *28*(5), 511-520.

Sonnentag, S. (2018). The recovery paradox: Portraying the complex interplay between job stressors, lack of recovery, and poor well-being. *Research in Organizational Behavior*, *38*. https://doi.org/10.1016/j.riob.2018.11.002

Stoeber, J., & Otto, K. (2006). Positive conceptions of perfectionism: Approaches, evidence, challenges. *Personality and Social Psychology Review*, *10*(4). https://doi.org/10.1207/s15327957pspr1004_2

Supian, N. S., Munajat, M., & Bukry, S. A. (2023). The effects of workplace office ergonomic intervention on work-related posture and musculoskeletal symptoms: A systematic review. *International Journal of Allied Health Sciences*, *7*(5).

Tang, Y. Y., Hölzel, B. K., & Posner, M. I. (2015). The neuroscience of mindfulness meditation. *Nature Reviews Neuroscience*, *16*(4), 213-225.

Terefe, S., Yazachew, L., Asmamaw, D. B., Belachew, T. B., Feleke, A., Tafere, T. Z., ...& Negash, W. D. (2023). Time management practice and associated factors among employees working in public health centers, Northwest Ethiopia: a mixed method study. *BMC Health Services Research*, *23*(1). https://doi.org/10.1186/s12913-023-10004-w

Trajkovic, J., Veniero, D., Hanslmayr, S., Palva, S., Cruz, G., Romei, V., & Thut, G. (2025). Top-down and bottom-up interactions rely on nested brain oscillations to shape rhythmic visual attention sampling. *PLoS Biology*, *23*(4). https://doi.org/10.1371/journal.pbio.3002688

Wajcman, J. (2019). *Pressed for time: The acceleration of life in digital capitalism.* University of Chicago Press.

Ward, A. F., Duke, K., Gneezy, A., & Bos, M. W. (2017). Brain drain: The mere presence of one's own smartphone reduces available cognitive capacity. *Journal of the Association for Consumer Research*, *2*(2), 140-154.

Watson, K. (2011). [Book Review] *Thinking, fast and slow*, by D. Kahneman. *Canadian Journal of Program Evaluation, 26*(2), 111–113. https://utppublishing.com/doi/pdf/10.3138/cjpe.26.010

Woolley, K., & Fishbach, A. (2016). For the fun of it: Harnessing immediate rewards to increase persistence in long-term goals. *Journal of Consumer Research*, *42*(6), 952-966.

World Health Organization (2019). *Burn-out an "occupational phenomenon": International classification of diseases.* WHO. https://www.who.int/news/item/28-05-2019-burn-out-an-occupational-phenomenon-international-classification-of-diseases

Zayas-Cabán, T., Okubo, T. H., & Posnack, S. (2022). Priorities to accelerate workflow automation in health care. *Journal of the American Medical Informatics Association: JAMIA*, *30*(1), 195–201. https://doi.org/10.1093/jamia/ocac197

Zhenjing, G., Chupradit, S., Ku, K. Y., Nassani, A. A., & Haffar, M. (2022). Impact of employees' workplace environment on employees' performance: A multi-mediation model. *Frontiers in Public Health*, *10*. https://doi.org/10.3389/fpubh.2022.890400

www.ingramcontent.com/pod-product-compliance
Lightning Source LLC
LaVergne TN
LVHW010652110826
845149LV00014B/3045

* 9 7 9 8 9 9 3 0 3 1 5 3 8 *